Political Risk Management in Sports

Political Risk Management in Sports

Warren Miller

CAROLINA ACADEMIC PRESS
Durham, North Carolina

ISBN: 0-89089-112-5
LCCN: 2001097411

Carolina Academic Press
700 Kent Street
Durham, North Carolina 27701
Telephone (919) 489-7486
Fax (919)493-5668
www.cap-press.com

Printed in the United States of America

Contents

Acknowledgments

It would be beyond my talents to acknowledge every person by name that had made this book possible. Nevertheless, I would be outrageously remiss not to give thanks to my wife, Marsha, who helped me organize my thoughts. I give thanks for my kids, Eleephra, Seesha, and David for putting up with me.

A very special thanks to Fletcher R. Lewis, my dear uncle, friend, and business partner for his experience and ideas about Empowerment.

Bob Ballatine, one of the best Pioneer/Innovator athletic directors I know, thanks for friendship, and to Von Washington, Jr., my most excellent example of the Positive Coach.

I would like to thank Mr. Jack Loudin and Bangor, Michigan for your demonstration of creative leadership.

I would also like to thank James DeSpelder of Middle Cities Risk Management Inc. for his friendship and lively talk about Risk Management and other things.

Special thanks to Dr. Herb Appenzeller for encouraging a new work and your help in making the book possible.

Thanks Dr. Georgia Johnson, M.D. for your helpful comments and research.

Foreword

Risk management has been an important part of the business and insurance industry for many years. Today risk management is a popular term that affects physicians and other medical personnel, bankers, investors, governmental officials, military strategists, meteorologists, managers of major projects, to name a few. George Head and Stephen Horn II writing in *Essentials of Risk Management* note, "in short, some kind of risk management exists for every type of uncertainty humans face."

The sport industry has now taken its rightful place in the evolution of risk management and it has become an important factor in the success or failure of a sport enterprise. Risk management, in the sport industry, affects everyone associated with sport such as the sport administrator, coach, athletic trainer, and owners of professional teams, governing bodies, participants and spectators. In the sports industry, one goal of risk management is to prevent unnecessary injuries and subsequent litigation in addition to developing a safe environment. Terms such as loss exposure, loss prevention, exposures to accidental loss, have become common in the sport industry.

Dr. Warren Miller, Ph.D., a sport management consultant, questions the lack of political risk management in recent textbooks. Dr. Miller addresses the most serious concerns of sport administrators as well as others who work as administrators — "how do I keep my job?" In *Political Risk Management* he adds a new dimension to the field of risk management — "the important implications of political aspects of risk management to risk management." Dr. Miller gets the immediate attention of his readers when he writes, "longevity to an athletic director is almost an oxymoron." From his surveys and interviews with athletic administrators, he reveals that 94 percent of athletic directors lose their jobs, not because of a lack of competency, but because of political failures. This alarming statistic describes the reason he wrote *Political Risk Management.*

Dr. Miller's book is a welcome addition to the Carolina Academic Press series of outstanding books on risk management and sport management. It is practical, easy to read, informative and after he discusses the problem, he offers solutions designed for any administrator in whatever area of administration. The book also targets coaches who find that a lack of political risk management is often more devastating than a losing record in their sport.

Political Risk Management is long overdue and is a "breath of fresh air" in the field of sport management. Anyone and everyone who deals with administration should have a copy of the book on their desk. It is essential reading if modern administrators hope to keep their jobs.

I congratulate Dr. Warren Miller for a breakthrough in risk management in the new century.

Herb Appenzeller
Executive-in-Residence
Sport Management
Graduate Program
Appalachian State University

Introduction

Politics is part of the everyday life of every professional in sports and management. Part of management and leadership responsibilities is the understanding and the management of *political dynamics*. What I mean by *political dynamics* is the political rules and principles and how they work on the job. It should be no secret to every college and high school athletic director and coach how political his/her job has become. Saying the right things but the wrong way and at the wrong time in the media or on the job usually has bad political implications. Sometimes the wrong action, or non-action, can quickly end a great position or career. As a sports and management consultant, I usually hear questions from angry, frustrated athletic directors and coaches: "I didn't have a clue that he was the board president's relative!" "Why didn't someone inform me about the rules of this crazy game?" "They were playing politics, but I did not know what to do?" As a result, I decided to write this book on political risk management in sports. I do not intend this book to be a study in political science, but to provide a new practical view of both old and new political principles as applied in sports management today.

Sporting events present the perfect demographic smorgasbord for some of our country's largest corporations. Where big money, management, and sports are involved, politics will always be involved as well. None would deny that the Olympic games are an international *political* sporting event involving millions of dollars. Professional sports and large universities make big money from their sports programs and there are political implications to these. Consistently winning high school sports programs also can create surprisingly strong revenues for a local community. However, once a community becomes dependent on these windfalls, any loss of these revenues becomes a political matter. A breakdown in the athletic program could reverse the fortunes of winning. Any loss of revenue will soon reveal the true nature of the political relationship—someone at the school is going to be corrected or fired!

The management of politics in sports is a real necessity. The successful professional recognizes this fact and strives to improve political skills to raise his/her level of success. What factors affect the internal political areas of sports management, and how to manage them, is the main theme of this book.

Some external political factors directly affect the lives of management, coaches, athletes and all those involved in sports and these factors are not always so obvious to identify. The health of national and local economies or changes in state and national political parties can affect schools. Nonprofit schools must receive the bulk of their funds from the state and local communities. When revenues are down, the lack of money usually hurts sports programs. Facility upgrades and increased coaching salaries can become low priorities when general finances are suffering.

In the 1980s, a number of small towns in the Midwest lost industries, devastating their local economies. Unexpected, yet related, problems surfaced. Many leaders moved away to better prospects, taking their families and leaving a huge void in the local community. A significant loss in community leadership and population can directly impact local sports programs. Decreased populations in smaller communities create a loss of students in local schools and less state revenue for schools.

Another difficulty is that many people intimately involved with the problems of schools cannot vote in bond issues and school board elections because they live in different towns. Teachers are an important voting group nullified in many Midwest small cities and towns by their absence in the community where they teach. As a result, sports programs suffer too. It is a sad phenomenon to see some cities bogged down in a financial depression while others prosper because leadership leaves one city for another.

Learning the subtleties of managing political relationships in sports is an on-going process for the Executive Director of Sports

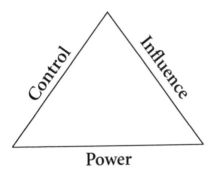

Power

Figure 1

Counseling Management Consultants. What affects money in sports will also affect the politics; that is the power, the control and the influence of money (see Figure 1). Our entire public school system must understand the need to search for new, innovative ideas that keep pace with the changing world of our children and their needs. My company is based upon this concept, to seek out and develop positive ways to innovate, educate and inform for the benefit of those involved in business management, sports management, and education.

Americans are the most political people in the world. We have rules for power, control, and influence as detailed and varied as any other country. We have many laws and procedures all derived from a complex legal and political system, yet without these political relationships, we could not have attained our current level of economics and global leadership.

Every day we make political decisions that have a direct impact on our lives. Make no mistake about it, politics play a significant part in the local political, social, economical, moral, and psychological health of our communities. Whenever power, control or influence is a factor in any relationship, we have a political relationship: a parent-child relationship is political; a coach-athlete relationship is political; an employer-employee is also a political relationship. Political relationships are not exclusive, but one of many relationships that occur together in any people-centered relationship. I designed this study to reveal the key elements that connect the internal political system with management and systems of Sports Management, using the ideas and models of empowerment.

Political Risk Management in Sports

Chapter One

Political Risk Management in Sports: Understanding Political Ideas

Our time is accelerating because the rate of change in receiving and developing information is accelerating thanks to the *Information Revolution.* We now have less time to solve more problems. In the 1990s, technology has discovered and produced more than any two other decades combined. The pressures to produce a winner are continually cutting in on developmental time. If he/she is lucky, the athletic director and coach will be given three years to produce a big winner, no matter the talent or system. Big money paid to top coaches and players has a price—*immediate production.* We cannot change the dynamics, but can offer some wisdom to respond.

When three or more persons attempt to work together, a political system automatically develops. Sports management, administrators and head coaches—any group will develop some kind of political system. Politics does not have to be a dirty concept used only by overly ambitious and amoral manipulators. People who refuse to understand or actively participate are simply deceiving themselves. Politics are the rules and force behind policy, communications, leadership, philosophy, accountability, planning, and advancement. Like it or not, it is inevitable in any workplace. Managing politics is part of any leadership and can be the boon or the scourge of every worker. I have heard medical doctors, teachers, preachers, and even a police officer declare their dislike of politics in their professions. Yet, politics is a neutral and, like most things, derives its positive or negative value from the motive of the user. Remember this: *In politics, what we do not know or understand is hardly ever passive concerning our safety and well-being in any political relationship or system.*

In surveys and interviews with coaches and athletic directors, we discovered that more than 94% of the firings or resignations of athletic directors and head coaches are caused by political failures. Surprisingly, the firings are not due to incompetence in their primary duties or job descriptions, but it is the parents of athletes in high schools and alumni at the college level who are the chief, though not exclusive, antagonists of athletic directors and head coaches. The implications are startling! Winning games or managing schedules is not enough to protect many professionals against losing their job, but failure to manage the politics of the job is often fatal.

> Successful management is essential to all segments of the sports industry, professional or amateur, school or club, private or government at any level, community or individual. Whatever the location of the management function, the same basic requirements are present: specifically, effective and efficient management of personnel, program, marketing, information, facilities, and legal responsibilities.

[Successful Sports Management, Herb Appenzeller, Guy Lewis (Introduction) by Guy Lewis.]

Below is a list of the six areas that management must manage successfully:

1. Personnel
2. Program
3. Marketing
4. Information
5. Facilities
6. Legal

No doubt, these are very critical to the success of any organization however, I would add one missing element — *managing political dynamics*. Each one of the listed six areas has interwoven political relationships. Failure to manage in any one of these six areas becomes a political failure for top management personnel and a risk management failure for the organization. Serious management and organizational failures will have political implications.

If leadership allowed uncontrolled infighting between important management personnel or mismanaged the conflict, the company could lose key personnel. Thus, poorly managed company politics becomes a risk management failure and, by default, a political failure. The company takes action. In the end, the justification for demoting or firing personnel will be the *perceived political failures*. In plain language, somebody made the organization look bad.

Political Terms

The following is a list of terms and definitions I use associated with politics in Sports Management that will be applied throughout this book.

1. A **Political Asset** is a positive term that can apply equally to both the person and the position. *Others always determine an employee's political worth as an organizational asset or liability.* Positive program achievements usually reflect at the least a temporary, workable political balance between the power groups.

2. A **Political Liability** is negative term that can apply equally to both the person and the position. *Others always determine an employee's political worth as an organizational liability or asset.* A political liability is considered a negative condition that reflects an unworkable balance between most of the political power groups.

3. **Political Adeptness** is the successful level of political problem-solving experience and political wisdom for achieving general and specific sports management tasks. This is a particularly skill needed by all three primary Sports Management leadership types.

4. **Political Posturing** is a deliberate political perception exhibited for the public that may or may not be true.

5. **Political Spinning** is the manipulation of facts, information, or events to create controlled perceptions, which may be partially true and always partisan.

6. **Empowerment** is the authorization to act through power, control, or influence. Understanding the empowerment of Power Groups is critical for achieving political safety, stability, and balance with longevity. Empowerment is divided into four main areas:

    - Personal Empowerment
    - Positional Empowerment
    - Political Empowerment
    - Legal Empowerment

7. **Truth, Beliefs, and Perception** are political ideas with related dynamics (for this study).

    a. *Truth* is any idea, fact, function, or principle that exists and operates independent of anyone's beliefs or perceptions. We understand truth as to levels and depths.

    b. *Beliefs* are the perceptions we accept. The quality of our knowledge, values, and motives largely determines our belief. The extent of our ability either to sympathize or to empathize with other people's ideas or circumstances will also influence our beliefs.

    c. *Perception* is what we are able to perceive. The quality and quantity influence our perception of sensory information, language, the influence of time, and our level of experiences or lack of experiences.

8. **Political Risk Management** is the process of understanding and managing political dynamics in the work place and planning against lethal political situations before they occur or as they happen.

9. **Political Responsibility** is a situation, events or persons we are totally accountable for *without* having total control or empowerment over them. It is a lever for political control and escape for those that have political responsibility over us.

10. **Policies** are interpreted political rules and procedures that are sometimes legal in planning. Good policies should reflect both political and risk management considerations as part of good leadership and management planning.

11. **Risk Management** is the process of making and carrying out decisions that will minimize the adverse effects of accidental losses upon an organization.[1]

12. **Political Power Groups** are the defined members of the total community that have some empowerment, directly or indirectly, on sports management. The specific identity of these groups varies from high school, college, and professional programs. As a rule, all school-level programs have similar members, though sometimes with different working dynamics.

13. **Applied Political Risk Management** is a model for problem-solving pre-existing situations or events through political management.

14. **Political Fires** are negative political situations or scenarios that need our immediate attention.

15. **The 2 + 2 Factors** is where unusual circumstance suspends normal cause and effect principles. Example: Hard work + good fundamentals + talent...should equal wins. Sometimes this is not true.

16. **Scapegoat** is any person, place, or thing that people blame for the failures of political responsibilities: time, the environment, my secretaries...are some more common scapegoats.

17. **Dynamics** literally means how things work in relationship to someone or something else.

18. **Crapulization** the attempt to justify or legitimize anything that is ridiculously inadequate or obviously bogus.

---

1. *Essentials of the Risk Management Process Volume 1* by George L. Head, Ph.D. and Stephen Horn, II, CPCU.

Chapter Two

College and Professional Leadership

Athletic Council and Board of Directors

Colleges and universities have an Athletic Council. Major decisions concerning the operation of the athletic program fall to this group. Working professors and experienced administrators with a positive interest in athletics usually compose the Athletic Council. The Board of Directors is the policy maker. Selections for this group are made from the community and chosen for their expertise in business, public relations, marketing, investments, and politics. The Athletic Council advises the collegiate athletic director and the Board of Directors advises the general manager in professional sports. Both groups are most effective when members are selected from a variety of education and cultural backgrounds.

The Athletic Council evaluates the performance of the intercollegiate athletic department and the Board of Directors evaluates the functions of the professional team. The Athletic Council and Board of Director's function are to counsel, not to interfere with, the daily operations. Daily program functions are the responsibility of the athletic director or the general manager. The highest-level administrators are politically responsible to their Athletic Council or Board of Directors. Councils or boards take responsibility for the planning of the organization. Both political and legal issues become the responsibility of the planners. Councils and boards protect the interests of the academic institution or in professional sports the owners and shareholders.

Political concerns should always be at the forefront of planning and policy setting which, therefore, makes them prime candidates for applying Political Risk Management. Athletic directors and general managers must be acutely aware of political concerns of the community. The need to know and the concerns and perceptions of power groups must be a high priority of sports management. Without the steady, strong support of the public success will always escape any program's long-term growth and success.

Athletic Director and General Manager

Both the athletic director and general manager have the responsibility for their staff and their job performance. In most systems, they decide the employment of staff members. Selecting staff is a serious political matter. In many high school systems, the secretary to the athletic director is one of the most important and visible secretaries in the entire system. The athletic department's secretary is often the first impression presented to the public from the athletic department. Therefore, making a careful selection for the right candidate is important. Unfortunately, many school districts do not appreciate or compensate this important position according to its merits. The amount and level of professional skills called upon by this position is considerable. I have always marveled at how administrations ignore or overlook the importance of this position. In some systems, clear bias is against fair compensation considerations for secretaries in the athletic departments, especially in many high schools. Every successful athletic director should have at least one competent full-time secretary.

When selecting personnel, political adeptness and positive attitude play an important role. Intercollegiate and professional sports are big business and are politically powered and managed. Much is always at stake, from huge monetary gains to prestige and high-profile employment opportunities. The management of business, the legal and the political implications, has made sports management a critical position.

Major Functions of the General Manager or the Athletic Director

1. Title IX
2. Public Relations
3. Managing
4. Training
5. Entertainment
6. Budget Preparation
7. Plan for Facilities Use
8. Building/Maintaining Facilities
9. Program Building
10. Security
11. Evaluating Coaches
12. Risk Management
13. Political Risk Management

The scope of the athletic director's position is rapidly expanding. In mid- to small towns across America, the health of the school's sports program has become closely associated with the general health of the community. Soft drink and shoe companies have marked athletic programs as important business targets. That alone should make school officials and parents alert to and aware of how important athletic programs are to outside groups.

Coaches and Managers

The coach works with the team and is responsible for its development. Head coaches are responsible for the total program. Assistant coaches have specific assignments and responsibilities that support the head coach.

The manager in professional sports is in charge of the organization and development of the team. Professional manager's duties and responsibilities are similar to those of intercollegiate coaches. Manager duties are, specifically, to improve the skills of individual players and mold athletes into a unified team, with the help of their assistant coaches.

Mounting legal responsibilities and the relentless political wars with parents is taking their toll on coaches as well as officials. Coaches of the 1960s and 1970s would not recognize, nor likely feel comfortable with, the coaching responsibilities of the post-1990s era. Tyrannical styles of coaching, especially in public school, are now almost certain lawsuits waiting to happen. Paperwork in athletic offices has tripled over the decade, according to some of the athletic directors interviewed.

Interestingly, an organization on the leading edge of positive coaching reform at the high school level is found in the state of Michigan. The Michigan High School Athletic Association (MHSAA) has taken the lead in promoting positive coaching and championing fun, safety, and sportsmanship for kids in sports. Jack Roberts, the current Executive Director, indicated plans for new leading edge, interactive workshops for coaches and athletic directors.

The Positive High School Coach

All coaches, like it or not, are role models, if not to kids, then to other coaches on other coaching levels. Survey information shows that many high school football, basketball, and baseball coaches model their coaching style after other level coaches (professional or college). Weekend coaches, like little league coaches, often pattern their coaching after upper-level coaches. For the coach, there is no escaping the role-model designation.

Coaching should be a challenging yet rewarding experience. However, coaching comes with a price and demands can strain family relationships as he/she gives, sharing the best of themselves with their teams, fans and other coaches.

Interestingly, the best former athletes often do not make the best coaches. It takes more than knowledge and a love of the game to be a successful coach. We must also include leadership, management, communication, and political skills, to name only a few, as must-have skills needed in today's coaching. The best coaches understand that the first burden of positive communications is their responsibility. Mastering the ability to adjust and adapt personal communications will be paramount in establishing a positive relationship with young teens. Poor recruiting and high player turnover usually suggests inadequate political relationships creating, poor communications. Charismatic personalities may draw young players to the program, but emotionally safe, fun, and genuine relationships keep players on the team.

Coaching at the high school, junior-high, and elementary level is radically different from coaching college or the professionals. Many high-profile professional and college coaches would make very poor high school coaches using his/her same philosophies. We are talking apples and oranges when comparing them. According to national surveys, the number one reason kids play sports is to have fun. This is not necessarily true for college or professional ranks, though many of these athletes do love the game. Good college coaches will recruit character and talent into their programs. In lower levels, the coach must *develop* positive traits he wants in his program. Winning and losing in colleges and professional programs can have serious financial implications. Professional and college athletes must bring talent and self-motivation to a sports program or face ouster. High school coaches face a variety of talent levels and motivational situations that are unavoidable. Then how do we balance between winning and having fun? Several common factors are found in every consistently successful amateur sports program:

1. Positive, progressive leadership that understands the positive benefits of a healthy athletic program for the positive development of athletes, school, and community with the willingness to commit to quality and innovation.

2. Broad, positive support from parents, administrators, teachers, the media, and the community at large (i.e., Power Groups).

3. Knowledgeable coaches with positive coaching styles that place kids first and winning second.

4. Elementary and junior-high programs that are valued and supported with good teaching coaches, as competent as those on the varsity team.

5. A genuine cooperation and commitment on the part of the coaches to work together for the welfare of the student athlete and with one another.

6. A community where good sportsmanship is wanted, appreciated, and rewarded.

7. A consistent system of fundamental training for athletic development in carefully controlled increments according to age, emotional maturity, and skill level.

My closing point is that people are positive assets and our children are the community's treasures. Politically smart winners are positive-thinking people who understand cause and effect. The first rule of cause and effect states that the first cause is *thought*. What we *think* eventually determines what we *do*. If we are thinking about every child's welfare, then we will act accordingly.

Chapter Three

Sports Political Power Groups

Definition: *Sports Political Power Groups are the specific groups within the total community that have some political empowerment directly or indirectly on sports management, athletes, coaches and its programs. The specific identity of these groups varies from high school to college and professional programs. Typically, all school-level programs have similar members, though sometimes with different group dynamics.*

Direct parental influence in high schools is different from parents with athletes in college programs. High school athletes are usually minors and that makes them legally influenced and, therefore, politically controlled by parents. College athletes are sometimes financially bound to their parents, though some students no longer have any political relationship with their parents on this level.

Obtaining an understanding of power groups is worth the time. Most of us can recall when we made the mistake of not considering all the people involved in a decision we made. This is not a wise move when it is necessary to manage an important political decision with important family or financial implications.

Getting in trouble with the boss is more complicated than it seems. An administration may have hired us, but we work for the entire community. This is the nature of the political system in public schools. Simply following the mandates of the board, superintendent, or principal will not protect the athletic director or head coach from becoming a political liability, resulting in firing. This is especially true if the administration is unaware or mistaken in the specific desires and commitment levels of the other power groups in the community that support the institution. Without the support and commitment of the local community, schools cannot function properly. Schools need the public as much as the public needs the schools. My research suggests that one of the biggest mistakes made by schools is not identifying or understanding and taking proper account of the empowerment of all the necessary power groups. Below in Figure 2 is a model of the typical public-school power groups.

Typical Power Groups

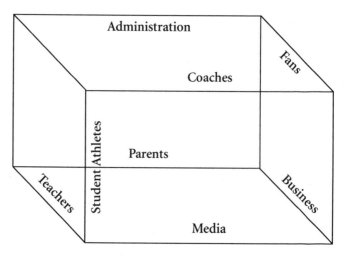

Figure 2

Parents are the most-feared power group in high school athletics for athletic directors and head coaches. In college, powerful alumnus groups take a center stage. Professional teams have to contend with sometimes-impatient owners, stockholders, the media, and the fans. People fear politics where knowledge of it is weak.

Maybe this description will be helpful in understanding the dynamic relationship between power groups and the athletic departments. Power groups are like parts of a living body with the athletic program at its heart. In a healthy body, all of the parts have a specific function but with the priority being the shared purpose of keeping the whole body alive. Notice I did not say the highest purpose is to keep the heart alive. The survival of the heart depends on the contribution of the other parts and, in return, the heart acts, pumping life back into the parts. If the health and welfare of the total body become the chief focus, this will ensure good health for the heart, along with all the other parts.

Coach Bobby Knight's problem with the Indiana University's administration and other public power groups is a good example of this principle. For a time, the university had made the coach the heart of the body. However, the problem was that the heart became the focus instead of the whole body with all of its parts. Eventually, the inevitable happened, the parts perceived that the heart was consuming more than it produced and became a political liability. The parts turned on the heart and destroyed it. To preserve the whole body, they got a new heart. This illustration may be a little dramatic, but I hope it made the point. We need each other to get the job done right. Anyone and any position can become a liability when the focus is misplaced. Bobby Knight could not make himself the focus, someone else did. Remember that someone always determines our political-worth as a liability or asset. People often misunderstand this dynamic.

When all the power groups are working together under the same philosophy, it is a beautiful thing. Nevertheless, when it fails, everyone suffers. For example, take the college booster program, that is not in accord with the athletic program, as it repeatedly violates school policy and NCAA rules to buy favors for athletes. They embrace the philosophy *the ends justify the means.* Yet, when discovered, this action earns the program and the entire school a very public rebuke. The athletic program will lose scholarships for future athletes and lose potential athletes to the program. Everyone loses and suffers.

Some school board members can represent more than four of the basic seven power groups as parents, fans, business owners, administration, and board members. Avoiding conflicts of interest is a critical issue for fairness and integrity for school board members. Because of these interwoven political relationships, Political Risk

Management is necessary. This group, school board members, represents the second strongest political power group to prove a danger to athletic directors, coaches and superintendents.

When the power groups are in an acceptable and happy balance, they will resolve many questions of control, power and influence. We must respectfully acknowledge empowerment from the most powerful to the least. Any one of these groups could be a potential land mine and must be properly addressed to achieve the balance as seen in Figure 3.

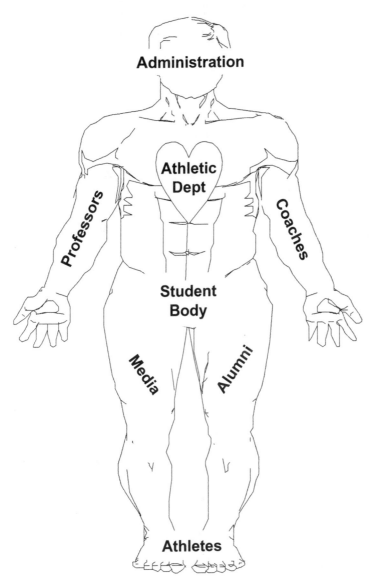

Figure 3

Chapter Four

Empowerment Levels

Empowerment is authorization to act through power, control or influence. I divide empowerment into four main areas:

1. Personal Empowerment

2. Positional Empowerment

3. Political Empowerment

4. Legal Empowerment

Personal Empowerment is what we bring to the job: our needs, beliefs, perceptions, truth, honesty, integrity, and codes. Many so-called professional politicians mistakenly promote candidates to fit the job. If a person is a weakling and a cheater, how will this condition change if given a position of power? This is the main cause for *abuse of power*. Would we want a job that demanded that all we believe be suspended and disregarded when working the job? Can anybody realistically accomplish this? Maybe if the person had a few redeeming qualities that might not be too severe, but what if the person is virtuous? Accepting these conditions weakens or nullifies personal empowerment when the position is more important than the person is. Somebody made this political decision. Think about it, when trouble comes, what is given priority, the position or the person? When the right match is made, we will see the person and the job as one.

If an honest man takes the office of President of the United States, then he will bring *honesty* to the position. However, if he were not honest, why would anyone expect him to be honest when he is President? The office of the President, or any other position of power, does not make the person. Would reasonable minds hire an average person to occupy a position that demanded a very smart person? Where would this person draw upon brilliance if not from inside? Again, the job does not make the person.

Schools sometimes hire teachers and coaches who do not like kids. Schools reason that a coach or a teacher must like kids. Cities hire police officers that habitually break the law. Sometimes, parents and coaches pressure big, non-aggressive children to play football when the child would rather paint. Women marry men who hate women. People should fit the job, especially if the job demands specific functions and traits. A customer service representative's job demands that they have a pleasant demeanor and be emotionally and verbally equipped to deal with people. If we cannot bring the traits necessary to job, the job cannot provide them. Personal empowerment is what we bring to the job. Personal empowerment sometimes demands we seek and excel as individuals through teamwork, but without losing or devaluing our selves. Faith, conviction, courage, and our own beliefs are part of our personal empowerment. Understanding our own empowerment is of the highest priority. Knowing our choices or options, both good and bad, will help us become a better person and a better leader. Some of our personal options are that:

- We can act or do nothing
- We can say yes or no
- We can delay and say maybe
- We can quit or continue
- We can innovate and use creativity
- We can take sides or stand neutral

Caught between a rock and a hard place is a scenario that we all have experienced. In the television series, Star Trek, they call this the *Kobayashi Maru* (no-win scenario). It was supposed to be a test for leaders to face and experience a no-win scenario. During a training session, the leader was placed on a simulated bridge of a ship in command of a crew. Star Fleet designed everything to go wrong and rigged the test so that no logical solution could be possible. All had to experience the taste of utter defeat. Captain James T. Kirk took the test twice and was the only person successfully to find a solution for the *Kobayashi Maru*. He broke into the computer and changed the conditions so that he would have a winning solution. Now some would say that he cheated and some would say he was brilliant. What do you think?

In real life, sometimes breaking through to change the parameters is the only thing to do. The reason we find ourselves pressed against the wall with no options is because we are accepting and operating needlessly in somebody else's program. Sometimes we need to find more information or develop more skills to get better options. Maybe we are working within somebody's too-narrow perspectives or beliefs. It could be that the towering walls all around us seem so high because we have not stood up and really considered their true measure. Fear distorts things making them look bigger and more ugly. Fear can make us sit when we need to stand or sometimes run instead of standing and holding our ground.

The fear of success or failure is a crippling condition that can hold anyone back, taking all who fear captive. Fear management requires honesty and acceptance of what we experience. Taking a positive attitude about our self will allow positive action in spite of fears. Eventually these fears, when we know their dynamics, will lose their grip and we can be free of them. The reason for the attainment of courage, on the personal level, lies in the benefit for all other empowerment levels. If we are courageous in personal empowerment, the other three-empowerment levels draw upon this courage. The source of your internal resources is within us. That is why the constant search and exploration of knowledge and wisdom are important. For many of us, the understanding and acceptance of God become our internal resource.

Undeniably, the best leadership is where leading by example is the model. *We must keep in mind that we cannot give what we do not have.* Our quality of knowledge, our values and our motives largely determines what we believe. Real knowledge and experience tells us we cannot believe everything, yet we must believe in something. Personal empowerment would demand that we continue to improve the quality of our knowledge and regularly seek to check our motives.

We should continuously develop our personal empowerment for it is the key to our own development as a person. Very successful, positive people have a strong, yet healthy sense of their own empowerment. Of course, we can use this empowerment for good or evil purposes. Understand that personal empowerment is what we brought to the job. The quality of life-motives will determine the long-range effect our empowerment will have on others. This empowerment belongs to us with complete ownership. Our personal empowerment is independent of the job. We bring our personal empowerment with us, everywhere we go.

Positional Empowerment

Now that we have established our personal empowerment foundation, we must explore our positional empowerment. The position or job we hold has its own empowerment, defined and granted by others. We must understand the boundaries. Our responsibility is to learn the boundaries of the position, even when they are not clearly defined. Find out what the last person in your position did or did not do. Ask your boss frank questions. The talent, experience, and political skill level of an individual may have an impact on the empowerment options in a position.

Empowerment is a political word. Power, and control and influence are all involved in getting the job done. The jobs own distinct use of power, control and influence will define that position. The athletic director or the principal's *given* responsibilities defines their empowerment level. In each case, someone else defined and granted the specific empowerment for that position. Sometimes through job descriptions or verbal and written mandates, leadership makes political decisions that establish the boundaries of our job empowerment.

The unprecedented presidential election between the candidates George W. Bush and Vice President Al Gore in Florida is the perfect example of confusing empowerment. Federal courts and state courts were all at odds about specific empowerment. Nothing will get a person in trouble faster than misunderstanding empowerment. Sometimes bad job descriptions are at the heart of internal troubles within organizations. Vague, contradictory wording can ignite a series of political fireballs that can bring down a company, organization, or individual. Because of this problem, a needed organizational position can suddenly become a liability to the organization.

For example, the administration fires the high school's first full-time athletic director because of intense external pressure caused by perceived political failures. The administration and school board are afraid of filling the position with another full-time professional athletic director. The group instead installs the part-time manager-type administrator instead of the needed innovator type and therefore the program suffers.

Sometimes personal empowerment and positional empowerment collide. The position empowers us to fire an employee for habitual tardiness. Yet, we know that this single parent has to get their child off to school, making them fifteen minutes late every day. What should we do? When a conflict develops, we must make serious, difficult choices. If keeping the job means losing our self, it is not worth the trouble. Your personal empowerment will determine the ultimate use of your positional empowerment. Someday we may have to say *I will not!*

Many have found the solution for unacceptable conflicts between personal empowerment and positional empowerment by self-defining both. We know such boldness as entrepreneurship.

Political Empowerment

Political empowerment is very closely associated with positional empowerment. However, skill and experience levels, and sometimes-even timing, will determine the scope of political empowerment. Political empowerment is using and understanding political dynamics to master a position. Learning to master political relationships is key to excellent management. Often, political adeptness directly relates to the longevity in a professional position by successfully managing the politics of the job. Having enough political knowledge, and understanding how and when to use it, translates into power. This power could include personal, positional, political and legal power.

Empowered with Political Risk Management can upraise an individual positively in a team environment. Yes, I said it! We can learn to safely excel as individuals in a team environment.

Two people with the same education, having the same job description, one becoming very successful and the other struggling, is an everyday reality. The difference is one not understanding and using political empowerment while the other did. I have developed Political Risk Management as a way to maximize the effect of managing politics, in a positive way, on the job. Understanding that politics is part of every job and every institution should lead most of us to want to understand and develop our own political abilities. Ignorance of office politics can, and eventually do, hurt us. Politics is seldom passive and what we do not know *will* harm us.

Equipped with knowledge of personal empowerment and armed with this understanding, we are ready to use political empowerment. Successful political strategies require experience and wisdom. Experience is first gained by our understanding and using the first two empowerment types (Personal Empowerment and Positional Empowerment). Wisdom will dictate the use of Political Risk Management. By working on our self first, we will learn some valuable dynamics that will help us work with others.

We clearly need other people and our relationship with others must be a positive one. The proper or improper use of political empowerment directly influences the quality and speed of communications and organizational flexibility to make timely adjustments and changes. The more people in the organization who are politically empowered, the better the internal communications and working relationships that directly influence the ability to make speedy changes. We must generate scrupulous motives when practicing power, control and influence. Negative presentations of power, control or influence will breed contempt. Cause and effect, working in others, can be very predictable when we understand the motives.

Successfully interpreting someone's motives requires that we are skilled at using empathy, able to walk a few miles in their shoes. Others' beliefs and perceptions can open to your understanding, thus making us most effective.

The negative idea of *payback* tempts everyone sometime during our lives. However, the problem with it is this, the operation of cause and effect. Throw out something negative and it will produce a negative effect. Our reputation should be precious to us. It directly affects others' perceptions and beliefs about our character and abilities. Remember we must always take the high road of truth in what we say or do. We have no legitimate needs for a defense against the truth; however, the truth can always challenge and defeat faulty beliefs and perceptions.

Legal Empowerment

Like the quote from an old Clint Eastwood movie *Dirty Harry*, "a man has to know his own limitations." We have to know our own legal position, especially in conflict. A legal solution will have an impact on every empowerment level. We always best temper legal considerations through the first three empowerment levels. Deciding later that we cannot live with our decision can be an awful burden to carry. Athletic directors and general managers have to be wise to know when to pull out the legal card. Future employment and long-range implications could devastate and quickly shorten a career. Once we make a matter public through the courts, the results may have unexpected consequences.

Sexual harassment and non-disclosure issues are making a big noise in the courts. Male coaches coaching female athletes and female coaches coaching male athletes should tread very lightly while the courts are still establishing clear legal lines. From fan rage to risk-management failures, Sports Management needs political management more than ever.

Stay current on the latest information targeted toward your profession. Subscribe to publications that directly affect your position. Be wise! Some actions may not be safe to do. Maybe another's situation was different at some key empowerment level, changing the dynamics. If in doubt, ask or research, seeking the truth. Avoid acting from fear, afraid to find out the truth. Of course, *we* know that the high ground of truth is the ultimate advantage in Political Risk Management.

Closing Thoughts

Here are some things we should never do in a *political* world:

1. Never sell your integrity for the money
2. Never fail to use Political Risk Management on the job
3. Never take on an advisor when we can have counselors
4. Never give away our personal empowerment
5. Never reward someone's incompetence
6. Never take the job just for the money
7. Never treat everyone equally...only fairly
8. Never refuse to take credit for your own work

Leave room for some error in your life. Mistakes are inevitable because, at best, we only know parts of anything. No one has the oversight over their own life or anyone else's and part of our best lessons comes from surviving mistakes. A positive attitude is often more important than aptitude, so avoid staying crushed when you fail. Immediately get back up and try again. The most successful and happy people I have ever known have failed and risen often. Here are some traits that I found in common with successful, happy people:

> Many of them believe in God
> All are not afraid to succeed or fail
> All are persistent, never giving up
> Love is in the center of their personal lives

Empowerment

Factors, both positive and negative, can influence the four areas of individual empowerment, personal, positional, political and legal.

In most leadership situations where no clear-cut answers to problems exist, these prominent factors can decrease the level of individual empowerment:

Fear of Failure	Fear of Rejection
Uncertainty	Placement of Blame
Unrealistic Demands	Compliant
Consequences of Actions	Second Guessing
Negative Responses	Fear of Success
Political Ignorance	

At the root of loss of personal empowerment by many leaders is the element of fear. School leaders such as principals, athletic directors, and superintendents have the authorization to act in critical situations, yet sometimes fear the consequences of exercising authority.

Case Study:

In a situation involving a high school district, the board of education authorized staffing cutbacks. The superintendent directed the principal to cut back a staff member from either the math or social studies department.

A cutback in the math department would involve the transfer of a low seniority female teacher whom they acknowledged was one of the best new teachers at the school. She was very popular with a power group of influential parents. This group wanted more emphasis on advance math classes.

The other cutback, in the social studies department, would involve the transfer of a social studies teacher, who was also the high school head football coach. Moving the coach could negatively affect the very successful football program.

The Parent Advisory Committee recommended that both positions face elimination and another solution be found. The teaching staff and the principal supported retaining the social studies position. This action would keep the football coach in the building. When asked for his recommendation, the principal stated his intention to retain the social studies position. However, the word leaked out to the academic-minded parent group. Immediately this parent group informed the principal that they did not agree with his decision. They informed him that they planned to go to the next board of education meeting to protest his decision. The principal talked with the superintendent. His superintendent assured the principal that he would support the principal's decision, keeping in mind the possibility that the board of education could reverse this decision.

Over the weekend, the principal received more supporting calls from parents who also wanted the math position retained. The following Monday the principal acquiesced and informed the school staff that he was reversing his original recommendation and would recommend the elimination of the social studies position.

This situation typifies a loss of empowerment out of fear for what might or might not have happened at the board meeting. Leaders often waste time focusing on things that they have no control over. The principal yielded to the pressure of the parents, fearing the consequences of his action, despite the support of the school staff and the superintendent. Perhaps the political concerns fueled a fear of a loss of parental support and he could not handle any challenges to his authority. Empowered leadership requires not only recognizing that the power is yours to use, but it demands courage. Political opposition will test the character of an empowered leader in situations where the answer requires judgment and accurate assessment.

Case Study:

In another situation, the superintendent instructed the administrative staff to accomplish the transfer of all children within four elementary and middle schools to other open schools in a too-short period. Only a few members of the administrative staff voiced their concerns about the unrealistic schedule. The superintendent asked the remaining staff if they felt they needed more time. Although the entire staff was aware of the idealistic assignment, the majority chose to remain silent, rather than expressing their honest views. Upon being dismissed from the meeting, most administrative team members openly complained about the unrealistic time deadline to each other.

Here the administrative team leaders were unwilling to speak out, fearing the possible wrath of the superintendent. No one wanted to be labeled a complainer nor did anyone want to seem incompetent or unprofessional. Perhaps some thought by not voicing their complaints, they had the appearance of a good team player.

Exercising empowerment requires degrees of mental, emotional, moral and physical toughness that enables a person to exercise control, power and influence. Empowered leaders can recognize negative influences and conditions of fear, doubts, and emotional burnout working in themselves and others. Understanding self creates a wonderful advantage in countering stress, loss of confidence, loss of self-worth, and diminishing effectiveness and we can successfully manage these factors once we recognize them. Our ability to succeed in most pressurized situations is proportionate to our individual empowerment levels.

Successful Empowerment Practices

Empowerment starts with self-renewal that includes:

Physical		Mental
Social	Spiritual Development	Emotional

This renewal process depends upon the situation, whether personal, positional, political or legal empowerment is at play. Personal success or failure is dependent upon awareness, knowledge, persistence, courage, and the ability to make adjustments accordingly.

Understanding that personal empowerment is vital to success, yet alone is not enough. Exercising empowerment in leadership situations can be difficult because of many factors. Achieving full personal empowerment involves the use of these terms in the following statements:

Imagination/Creativity is the ability to extend resource potential (i.e., time, personnel, ideas, facilities, etc.) and allows for the exploration of creative possibilities. This is important in becoming an empowered individual. In critical or even life-threatening situations, people often fail or die because they panic. When people panic, they stop thinking about the creative possibilities that could change the dynamics of any situation to the positive. The empowered individual strongly wants to be confident, levelheaded and clear thinking. Quantity and quality of our thinking have a direct impact on how we act. Creativity can overcome the lack of other needed resources. Only through imagination can we truly explore the limits of our resources.

Self-awareness allows for the consideration of our own alternative possibilities. Understanding our strengths and weaknesses as a leader can make us more secure when treading in new territories of experience. Just as the adage says, "there is more than one way to get to Philadelphia," an empowered individual can look for alternative questions and solutions without fears. Positive self-talk will reinforce our internal positive-thinking processes. When we know whom and what we are, how becomes very manageable. Self-aware people understand the need and cost of change when adjustments are necessary. The realities of the cost involved in changes and the rewards of growth and success are never too expensive to the self-aware person. Self-aware people take responsibility for what they say and do. Change is internal and external and we are not responsible for changing others, yet we may provide encouragement. The person who understands their own awareness knows that all things living must change and is the dynamic way of our world. Change, to those who understand, becomes something to appreciate.

The empowered individual leader must exercise personal empowerment to be successful. Taking personal responsibility for what we allow to happen to ourselves is necessary for political survival. In many work situations, leaders take on burdens and problems that they have the power to reject. Learning which is which and when to accept or reject responsibility becomes the test of our political adeptness.

On the field of play, defeat does not mean that we must fail in other parts of our lives. Setbacks or defeats do not define who or what we are. Sometimes going with the flow may be wrong. Empowered individuals do not allow others to decide how much and what is important to them.

Good leadership requires *sound judgment* to meet the needs of both individuals and the group fairly. Leaders face certain situations where the answer is not readily apparent. In work situations, occasionally an individual may have mental, emotional, or physical problems that will not permit them to function in a group setting. The time spent meeting the needs of the one individual may or may not be fair to the remaining larger group. Sometimes the rights and needs of the individual are greater than the whole. A leader must make a judgment on these issues.

In the *Kobayashi Maru* (no-win scenario), Star Trek's Captain Kirk broke into the computer room and changed the rules to win. When Mr. Spock, known for his logic, faced with the *Kobayashi Maru*, he chose personal sacrifice as his solution. He reasoned that in his situation *the needs of the many outweighed the needs of the few, or the one.* He laid down his life for his friends. Every leader will make important decisions based on moral, political, social, or ethical principles, balancing the needs of the individual and the needs of the organization.

Insight and Wisdom is what a good leader eliminates much self-defeating behavior with. Even so, leaders often fall prey, attempting to do and be everything to everyone. We must view both good and bad positively, which will eventually yield experience, then wisdom.

We must not be afraid to make errors. Even bad mistakes and failures are great opportunities for learning. While information may change, wisdom remains. Seek wisdom!

Humor is the ability to see the lighter side of situations and is precious. Laughter brings joy to the spirit, releasing endorphins, making our bodies feel good. The empowered leaders who use humor keep things in perspective by not allowing problems and situations to destroy inner peace. For every problem, a potential solution can be found. When unwanted tension threatens to destroy a meeting, genuine humor can be used as a way to dissipate negative feelings. Sometimes laughing at our self clears the negatives from our own attitude.

Chapter Five

Selecting the Right Person for the Right Job

It is critical that both the candidate and the interviewers ask and discuss political matters in any interviewing process. The chances are that sufficient athletic knowledge and administration skill has qualified the candidate for the interview, yet, is the candidate politically experienced and astute enough to survive the political responsibilities of the job? As an administrator, are we hiring the right person for the right job? Do we understand the necessary political skill levels of the professionals that we are hiring? Can our candidate withstand the political pressures and challenges in our particular work place or community? What are the consequences of hiring the wrong candidate to the program and us? If we are the candidates, have we done our homework well enough to know the political climate that we will be walking into? Seeking out and understanding the complete nature of the political implications is using Political Risk Management.

Avoiding the wasteful revolving-door policy of hiring and firing of athletic directors and coaches is expedient. Habitual personnel changes destroy any kind of positive program continuity. Those that continually approve the wrong candidates will seem incompetent to the public. The leadership must successfully identify needs and wants, then agree and develop a process to choose the right candidate, using Political Risk Management.

Who would hire a dentist to do a triple bypass on a family member? Unfortunately, this is what typically happens when schools hire key personnel in Sports Management. The tragedy is that neither the candidates nor the administrators really know what is needed to get the job done. How many people are now working for a boss that is a complete affront to their way of thinking, making the job miserable? How many employers are lamenting the day they hired an employee that seems a catalyst for political fires. It is understandable why so many athletic directors in high schools and head coaches in college and general managers in professional ranks have such a high turnover rate.

When Power Groups are not working together as a team, the usual end is failure, anger, and political fires. Without a specific *shared vision* programs drift, all parts going in multiple directions. Who really should be accountable for achieving this common vision? Political Risk Management demands all parties be responsible.

Specialization in Sports Management

The Information Revolution is making substantial impacts on how sports management does its business at every level. By speeding up the rate of change and shortening the rate of receiving information, faster information places more pressure to produce more in less time. Coaching and administration experience does not solely qualify a successful candidate for an athletic director in most programs as in the past. Legal, business, and political implications, and the increased pressure for excellence, with full-media communication responsibilities and public relations expectations, have considerably expanded the scope of the position. The public, including business, is acutely aware of the generating power of sports programs, making sports management positions increasingly more important to institutions.

Sports Management Specialists are increasingly manning athletic programs. Increasing demands and the growing importance of sports to schools and communities make it almost impossible for one person to fulfill every program need for very long. An emerging pattern of specialized program management development is emerging on all levels of sports. *Leadership type* must not be confused with *personality type*. The leadership type is concerned with what specific, tangible skill is used in the profession. How they express these skills is more the personality type. Listed below are the three main Sports Management leadership types and their profiles. A working knowledge of these types is essential for making the right employment decisions.

The Pioneer

- Pioneers are great organizers who can create programs and facilities from scratch or can take leadership in major facility-renovation projects.
- Pioneers make ideal candidates for new athletic and recreation program development.
- The best candidate will have good general writing and speaking skills, with excellent business and political skills.
- Usually leaves to start or build another fledgling program.

The Innovator

- Innovators bring a strong philosophy to the program, increasing efficiency. An Innovator will bring the program to its highest performance level, based on available and pledged resources and how much support from community power groups.
- The Innovator can hire, train, and develop skilled program-building personnel with sound teaching fundamentals and deploying leading-edge techniques for developing personnel at all levels.
- The Innovator has the skill to identify cause-and-effect problems and repair weak programs, while increasing athletic participation, infrastructure usage, and staff efficiency.

- Innovators will display excellent political and interpersonal communication skills when working with their staff and the power groups.

- Pure Innovators will leave while the program is still peaking, rarely staying longer than three to five years.

The Program Manager

- Program Managers usually assume leadership after the Innovator, maintaining the same strong, successful program without making major changes.

- Politically adept mangers will strengthen communications and involvement with the power groups. Coaches and staff will stay encouraged with minimum interference.

- Program Managers will stay current with the latest leading-edge equipment and ideas.

- Managers stay if he/she can maintain current and expected levels of success. Properly using Political Risk Management and Legal Risk Management principles can help add years to the job.

- The Manager has excellent speaking and writing skills.

Study the intersecting circle diagram in Figure 4. Note that the Pioneer intersects with the Innovator and the Innovator intersects with the Manager. This tells us that some overlapping of skills is inevitable and can be very helpful. However, the Pioneer type and the Manager type have no logical overlapping of skills. It is a disastrous situation when administrations hire the Manager to do the job of a Pioneer. Turning the Pioneer loose on the job of the Manager is equally dangerous. Remember we are not talking about the personality type, but the leadership type. Any type will have a variety of personalities.

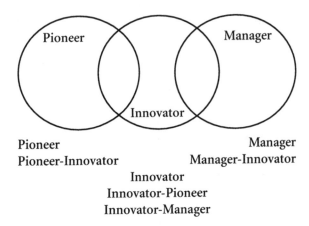

Pioneer   Manager
Pioneer-Innovator   Manager-Innovator
Innovator
Innovator-Pioneer
Innovator-Manager

Figure 4

Specialization—
More Attributes

The Pioneer

Pioneers will be high-energy individuals. They organize well and are politically effective at generating positive public relations for finding community support in initial program-building stages. Look for a strong, task-orientated person with competent business and leadership skills who has a record of developing strong athletic foundations and infrastructure, in similar-size systems. Because of the vast experience and strong skill levels needed, the pure Pioneer is harder to find. The Pioneer will have excellent experience and knowledge of facilities acquisition and program maintenance procedures. High moral and ethical reputations are common traits of successful Pioneers. The broader-skilled Pioneer person could temporarily do the work of the Innovator. This transition can be very logical in some systems. Sometimes when incompetence has devastated a program, schools must hire the Pioneer to rebuild. The sudden growth of a program could also call for the Pioneer's craft.

However, his/her strongest and most productive skills will define him/her foremost as a Pioneer.

The Innovator

Successful innovators will win over the community eventually and be credited as the savior of the program. This probably is not fair to the Pioneer, but many people see it this way. Participation at all levels in and out of the program will increase under his/her dynamic leadership. Changing agenda can best suit Innovators to accomplish needed coaching changes. The Innovator's installation of a strong sports philosophy will include the desires and commitment levels of the institution and the community. Innovators seek better cooperation and efficiency. The positive Innovator will expect personnel to work closely together as a united unit with a common philosophy. Innovators can become mentors to young or new coaches, successfully work, and encourage the more-experienced coaches.

The Innovator will seek stronger financial commitments from the administration and community. Coaches will show the highest level of achievement under the Innovator's leadership with the available resources. Feelings of shared ownership by the community will unite the community.

Innovators will be visionaries armed with tangible practical skills, knowledge, strong leadership skills, and equally strong verbal skills. Positive Innovators can comfortably gather other talented people around them without fear or jealousy, strengthening the program. The Innovator leader is usually the most many-sided leadership type (Innovator-Pioneer, Pure Innovator, Innovator-Manager). Experience, skill, and personality vary greatly among this group. Consideration to program details and personnel needs should dictate which leadership-combination type the organization hires.

The tricky part for the Innovator is balancing the realities of resources and the commitment level of the school and the community. A leader without followers is probably moving too fast, too slow or failed to prove the vision. Innovators in the public school setting must keep a sensitive eye on the responses and reactions of the school and the community to his or her innovations.

The downside of these versatile, innovating individuals is that they run the greatest danger of becoming a Negative Innovator. Negative, but talented, Innovators can successfully build up programs, but often the cost will be very great to the entire program and community. These task-orientated individuals will demand much more hands-on control with weak delegation of authority to others. Total control without accountability, other than judging their winning percentages, has cost many universities and schools years of rebuilding after the Negative Innovator leaves. Negative Innovators always use tyrannical approaches. One way to identify Negative versus Positive Innovator leadership is to observe what happened to the programs after the Innovator left. How healthy is the program and is there a strong, successful foundation for the Manager type to take over? Has the Negative Innovator devastated the program legally, politically, financially, or ethically making it necessary for the program to go back to the Pioneer's leadership?

Negative Innovators seem like the right answer when power-group pressure is mounting on the administration to produce a winner in short order. However, quick gratification using the Negative Innovator can have negative, long-range implications as its cost. The responsibility rests on the administration that sought and hired the Negative Innovator. Sometimes even the Negative Innovators have their uses if somebody is really able and willing to pay the cost. That first championship is the greatest hurdle to any program and, to some institutions, the needed catalysts for future championships. This can be very true in professional and college sports like football or basketball, to name only two. Once a school births a champion, recruiting talent for both coaches and athletes gets a lot easier and productive.

Staying too long in a position is possible for the Pure Innovator. Constant innovation would be too taxing for most institutions. Emotional energy and the time required for perpetual change would eventually seriously weaken the potential of the program and staff. This type of changing would leave little time for needed development. Sometimes a program moving in the positive direction moves too quickly, changing important political dynamics, affecting coaching personnel. The Innovator, if successful, will eventually innovate themselves out of a Pure Innovator's job. If the Innovator has management skills, he can make the smooth transition to Innovator-Manager. I have observed a particular problem that younger Innovators incur more often than with other types. In consideration of their own children, Innovators sometimes stay too long in the system. Athletic directors with older families are sometimes reluctant to move. Family dynamics for professional athletic directors seem to move in extremes. The family either is unusually strong and close or is teetering daily in crisis. The pressure of performance and the pressures of constant moves and new starts take a toll on the best of athletic directors and their families. Think about it! Many athletic directors and their families move every three years, looking for a new job, in a new city, and leaving friends behind.

The Program Manager

Politically astute with very competent management skills, the Program Manager will become the glue to weld and maintain the program's current successes created by the departed Innovator. The position demands an intelligent problem-solver who will strengthen the relationship between the power groups.

The Program Manager must be an excellent public speaker for the athletic department with good, sound business and multimedia skills. Clever scheduling and positive public relations will become important tasks of the Program Manager. Meeting the challenges to maintain current program successes will prompt new, timely small upgrades and advancements to keep the program on the leading edge. Monitoring and encouraging the continuing education of all coaches in the system will be important. Maintaining the integrity of the current winning program philosophies makes political sense. When a successful Innovator suddenly leaves a program, the Program Manager makes a good interim replacement.

Weighing the particular type of leadership needed at any stage is important. Some programs may have mixed needs. Maybe the men's program requires more of the Program Manager's skills and the women's program needs the Innovator-Pioneer. Of course, the priorities of program needs must be properly determined before hiring any type of permanent leadership (see Figure 5).

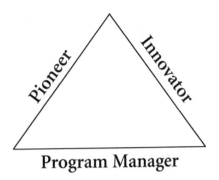

Figure 5

Often people doing the hiring of sports management personnel do not understand their real program or personnel needs. Nor do sports management candidates understand the importance of Political Risk Management in their quest for a position. The ideal situation is for the employers to want what they truly need. Wanting something other than what we truthfully need is very wasteful and politically dangerous. Superintendent, principals, and school boards are usually just as uninformed of today's sports management as anyone is. Complicating matters, more are athletic directors, general managers and head coaches taking jobs that poorly suit their strongest talents and accepting jobs that will exploit their weakness. Political considerations are just as important as the job skills, opportunities and the money.

Make certain to do all your homework and find out what political troubles the previous person had on the job. Discover if they view the position sought as an asset or a liability and by what power groups. Are the goals stated by the screening committee the same as the written job description that originally attracted our attention? Have we met and do we like the person that we have to report to if selected? Will our management-type skill or personality clash with key people on the job?

Those smiling faces looking at us over the interviewing table may not have our specific welfare as high on their priority list as we do. Armed with the knowledge of Political Risk Management employers and employees can jointly avoid making the wrong choices.

It goes without question that the professional using Political Risk Management must understand his or her own abilities and empowerment first. Chances are, if the money is right, but the politics are very wrong, we will not enjoy the money or be collecting it for very long.

Leadership-Type Impact on Coaching

The wrong leadership type in sports management personnel will have serious repercussions on the coaches in the program. Inexperienced coaches with zero to three years need the Pioneer-Innovator type leadership to establish and develop them and their programs. Team building is relatively simple and selfish compared with the benefits of program building. Programs can only sustain long-term success through thoughtful program building. Energy, time and training must be directed to the coaches to meet their needs. Coaching in the millennium will require better skills, more knowledge and less time for development than in the previous decade. Program-building coaches differ from team-building coaches. A successful program can replace and replenish coaching needs with team building coaches. Management must seek the right skills for the program.

Successful coaches with more than fifteen years of experience will flourish best under the Manager-Innovator type, with the emphasis on the Manager type. Political fires can easily flare when the wrong leadership type clashes and negatively affect an existing successful program. However, if the "old-timers" stop winning, the Innovator may have to help rescue the program.

For a new athletic director, understanding the experience and success levels of the existing coaching staff is critical. An inexperienced athletic director or head coach, with the wrong leadership type, in charge of a staff composed half of successful veteran coaches and half with young new coaches will probably fail. Experienced, successful coaches will respond to the management style of the athletic director and will resist too many changes in the system, especially if they are winning. The inexperienced coaches need more time and help to learn how to build complete programs. Politics and time management can destroy some inexperienced athletic directors.

Working with coaches requires much time and energy of any athletic director. Having an extreme coaching staff to work with would probably be too much for the inexperienced athletic director. The positions of athletic director and head coach are increasingly allowing less time for on-the-job learning and development. The pressures of producing quick-winning programs discourage the slower professional development in sports that were allowed in the past. This is no secret to the coaches in professional sports, like football and basketball, where every year your job may be up for grabs. The once reliable five-year plan is obsolete, in today's impatient reality. Leadership must produce in two or three years what they were previously allowed to do in five.

Coaches represent a powerful power group that leadership must take into political consideration. Athletic directors should hire and assign head-coaching assignments according to leadership types and program needs. Careful selection of head coaches by the athletic director could have an immediate impact on recruiting better athletes. Figures 6 and 7 represent the mixed needs of a typical athletic department. Note the match-up between individual program needs and the type of leadership.

Innovator/Pioneer

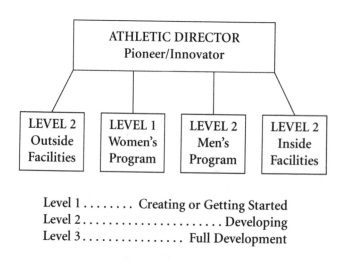

Level 1 . . . . Creating or Getting Started
Level 2 . . . . Developing
Level 3 . . . . Full Development

Innovator/Manager

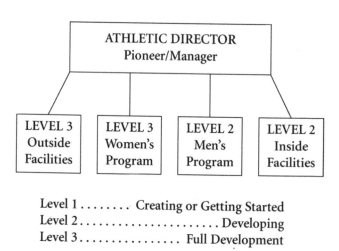

Level 1 . . . . Creating or Getting Started
Level 2 . . . . Developing
Level 3 . . . . Full Development

Figure 6

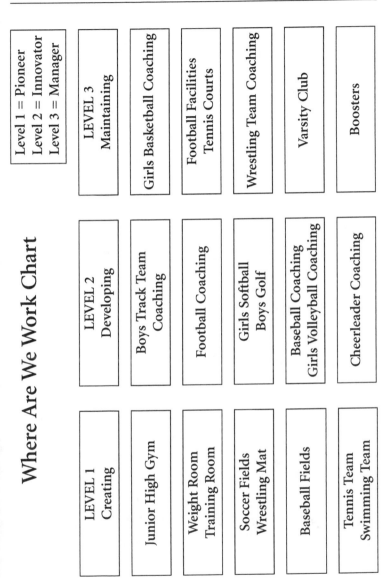

Where Are We Work Chart

Level 1 = Pioneer
Level 2 = Innovator
Level 3 = Manager

LEVEL 1 Creating	LEVEL 2 Developing	LEVEL 3 Maintaining
Junior High Gym	Boys Track Team Coaching	Girls Basketball Coaching
Weight Room Training Room	Football Coaching	Football Facilities Tennis Courts
Soccer Fields Wrestling Mat	Girls Softball Boys Golf	Wrestling Team Coaching
Baseball Fields	Baseball Coaching Girls Volleyball Coaching	Varsity Club
Tennis Team Swimming Team	Cheerleader Coaching	Boosters

Figure 7

Chapter Six

Coaches Conundrum

Coaching must change with the rapidly changing lives of student athletes, parents, and even the game. Children adjust to the rate of change more easily. However, adults have to adjust their mind-set to stay informed, consciously working to stay teachable. The initial responsibility of communication is always with the teacher and the coach. As adults, sometimes we forget how sensitive we were as kids to phony relationships with adults. Kids know when coaches are coaching just for a paycheck or self-promotion. Today's kids will believe and commit to a political relationship only after observing and believing in the professional and personal life of the coach.

When interviewing coaches that have practiced their trade more than two decades, most conceded to not having the same impact on their athletes as on past generations of athletes. Many coaches cited the general changes in kids. Kids knew more at an earlier age and communication was more difficult. The generation gap in coaching is real. Old-timers also say the new generation of coaches is much more aggressive and has many more hi-tech toys, but is less patient. However, the past and present are now clashing. The past must yield some things to the present. Coaches who cannot adjust mentally and politically will be forced out of coaching. Unfortunately, the stakes have risen in all levels of sports. Owners and fans are increasingly impatient for wins, leaving less time for professional development for both coaches and athletes. Particularly in professional and college coaching, a winning record, playoff, and post-season appearances provide no job security. *The Five-Year Plan* by J. Phillip Roach is now down to the three-year plan. Five-year goal achievements must now be completed in three years. High school sports cannot be far behind.

Warning signs for a coach would be his/her inability to form and maintain positive relationships with kids and their parents. Kids will rebel if forced to return to a past reality that is only in the coach's experience. I think that the lack of sufficient common experiences between adults and children is at the heart of the current generation gap.

Political Risk Management Parent Guidelines for Coaches

Properly understanding and addressing parental empowerment is critical! Parents represent the other third of the political relationship that exists between coach and athlete and parent and athlete. Political Risk Management positively manages the political relationships so that relationships may function to benefit every party (especially the athlete).

The burden of positive parental political relations rest first on the sports management professional and the administration on every level (school board, administration, athletic director, and head coach). Nothing will get one roasting in a political fire faster than failing to properly respect parents of student athletes. We must help parents to define their positional empowerment role in the program. Most parents are reasonable when they understand up front what the coach and their child needs of them. Left to their own designs, some parents will either move toward assisting too much or not contributing enough. American family dynamics is more complex now than in the past, making communication much more difficult. Increasing single-parent issues complicate the coach's needs to establish the coach/parent relationship.

If we can give parents some necessary guidelines about how they can help, this increases the chance to construct a positive coach-parent relationship that will benefit everyone. Parents, for the most part, want to make a positive contribution to their children's athletic life. When conflict erupts between the parent and coach, the parent wins the power struggle. Do not give up on single parents! The extra time and effort to establish a relationship with this group can be very rewarding to all parties.

Instruct Parents never to put their child in the middle of a parent/coach conflict. Disagreements with coaches happen. Still, if handled wrongly, it can result in parents venting to their child about the coach's strategies or team rules at home. Talk with parents at the beginning of the season; invite them to talk *directly* to you if they have a problem. If they think that their child is not getting enough playing time, show them your written and signed team covenant—the covenant explains the goals, responsibilities, and rule for the team (see the section on *Team Covenants* for more information). Show them where the team as a whole agreed on this matter. The coach must explain to parents the purpose of the team covenant. Give the team printed copies of the covenant to share with their parents.

Parents Need Access. Parents with direct access will be less likely to discuss their dissatisfaction behind your back with other parents. A lack of foresight in developing a parental response system could lead to sudden lethal political situations. Parents are not our enemy, but coaches must respect them. Failing properly to account for parental empowerment could be the catalyst for your political downfall. The high ground of truth is to know and believe that the needs of the child must come first with reasonable attention to parents.

Parents want and need a way to express their feelings and concerns where their children are involved. Some emotional parents share their children's athletic victories and defeats to surprising extremes. These parents can be very unpredictable and potentially dangerous. Good coaches help their team through crushing defeats. Who helps the parents? Hurts left untreated can lead to anger, which could then develop into deep-seated bitterness or into depression. Making opportunities for releasing emotions can help parents to cope with the needed dissipation of the extreme emotions generated through athletic competition.

Without some kind of effective closure, both the athlete and parent may suffer some emotional damage. I have treated clients and parents of athletes, unable to cope with what I call *Emotional Fan Stress Syndrome*. Upset stomachs, headaches, sleeplessness, and anger building to sudden rage are some symptoms I have observed. Sometimes the spouse and other children are the recipients of this type of parental rage. Coaches or officials, if available, will be the primary targets. Some parents agonize with extreme empathy with every missed tackle or blocked shot. Blood pressure elevated to almost dangerous levels, squealing and groaning over each crunching hit on the field. Some of these men and women would love nothing better than coming down from the stands to suit-up and go in and hit somebody.

Case Study:

> One year, at the Michigan High School State Wrestling Tournament, I bumped into an athlete and his father about an hour before the finals began. The wrestler and I had been friends since he entered high school. He had made the finals and was to battle against the defending state champion. The year before he had been third and I predicted he would be the winner the next year. Both were nervous. The tension was thicker than corn syrup in a cold cupboard. The wrestler's father was an older man and his appearance worried me. I spoke a few encouraging words to the wrestler and he seemed to relax.

> Over coffee with the father, I discovered that the stress was taking a toll on a man already very ill. No one else seemed to have noticed the shaky hands and the courageous tears barely held back. Before his son's match, we chatted and laughed until we were giddy. During the match, a very closely contested contest, he began to tighten up again. His hand would slide up to his chest. He was not aware what he was revealing. His son and the reigning champion wrestled the match of their young lives. In the end, the referee held

his son's hand high in the air. The triumphant father grabbed my hand and held it as tears of joy dripped from his face. Later he told me that his fears had been overwhelming him and that our chance meeting in the stadium may have prevented a heart attack. Today whenever he sees me, he greets me with a tap to his chest.

Divided Loyalty and Confusing Empowerment engineered by the parent can seriously damage the sporting potential of his/her child. Often, we put players into a no-win scenario, trying to please both the coach and the parents during practices and during games. Even if the parent's suggestion is a useful one, having the parent yelling out instructions in the middle of a game may not be helpful to the athlete. A hesitation in competition in some team sports could result in serious injury or sudden defeat.

Case Study:

> While attending another high school wrestling tournament, I witnessed such an event. Nearing the end of a highly contested match, the favored wrestler had scored a spectacular escape to tie the match. Throughout the match, the guy sitting next to me would holler instructions to the wrestler. I correctly deduced that this was the wrestler's father. I found out later that the father had been a successful high school wrestler and had been supporting and coaching his son throughout his career. The team's wrestling coach was well known and highly respected.

> The father's voice carried easily to the mat and his son was obviously listening. I caught the subtle wincing of the coach whenever the father commanded a particular move. With only ten seconds left in the match, tied three to three, the coach instructed his wrestler to use a series of arm-drag techniques. These techniques were safe and prevented stalling penalties. It was obvious to me that the coach now wanted the match to go into overtime. The coach knew that his wrestler was in better physical condition and would have the advantage in overtime. The wrestler's father literally screamed out his displeasure at this tactic, berating his own

son's effort. He commanded with all the authority of a man who knew his son, to shoot a single-leg takedown. I could see the confusion on the wrestler's face. Between the stolen look at his insistent coach and then into the stands, he hesitated. Meanwhile, the other wrestler took advantage of the hesitation and suddenly threw him to his back and won just before the last second expired in the match.

Parental Support is the most important thing a parent can give. It is a positive move to be there for the athlete to support him/her at home. Competitive sports can be incredibly stressful to players, no matter the skill and talent level. The last thing any athlete needs is a personal critic ranting and raving at home. Tell parents what their role should be for the athlete at home. Ask parents to be the encourager and provide the safe emotional haven. The coach wants parents to focus on the positive things their child is doing and leave the coaching to the team coaches. Make it clear that, especially in team sports, everyone's actions have an impact on the outcome of a contest.

Case Study:

Working as a Sports Counseling consultant for a high school, I encountered this situation. A talented, but new basketball coach was desperately trying to turn around the failing basketball program that he had inherited. In fact, the entire sports program was in shambles and most teams were experiencing habitual losses and the general attitude of the fans was negative. The coach heroically began to lift the program to a level of respectability.

One of the better athletes on his team was a three-sport athlete. His family was avid supporters of athletics. During the middle of their season, this athlete began to digress in his ability to control the ball. His shooting percentage plummeted and his turnovers were skyrocketing. The coach came to me and asked me to speak to his student athlete. The student and I met in an empty room at the school and I questioned him for about twenty minutes before I understood the nature of his problem. His father, a very prominent member of the community, and another member of his family were pressuring the athlete at home. The family seemed calm enough at games, but at home, the family analyzed his every move and linked his sports performance with their esteem for him. Every missed shot and every failed pass became an agonizing self-exclamation of the athlete's self worth. The athlete bled with every missed opportunity and turnover. The family would embarrass him as they openly began blaming his coach for his failures.

This athlete was another victim of *Winning-by-Proxy Syndrome* (*Sports Psychiatry* by Daniel Begel and Robert W. Burton). After a couple of sessions, he could get through the season with a small amount of added encouragement. Once he understood the dynamics of his problems, he decided to help himself. He graduated and moved away to college to get professional help.

Parental Sportsmanship in the stands can make the difference in a close game. The political implications of sportsmanship could be very positive or disastrous to the entire community. Visitors to your community will judge your community by your public actions or lack of action.

Particularly in mid-sized to small communities, athletic events are big social events. Representatives from all areas of the community are usually present. Classy fans or foul-mouth grumbling fans will leave an impression. Unfortunately, this negative group will speak for the entire community. Sure, not everyone is guilty of negative behavior, but if standards are so low that the community regularly and openly permits such bad manners, it will speak volumes. This too, speaks to the tolerance of the whole community seen through the perception of business and potential young families to the community.

Some of the worst violators of good sportsmanship in the stands have been community leaders in towns I have visited. In one city, the president of the board of education was inches from a fistfight in the stands at a high school football game. Face-to-face he stood yelling at another parent over field tactics. In one game, a well-respected citizen in a small community picked a fight with the visiting basketball coach.

Providing the home advantage is one of the simplest, but most effective things to do. It is good thinking to ask parents and the community to help create the perfect home-court advantage. Explain the advantages and how the team needs their unity and spirit. Once they understand, hopefully they will become a relentlessly positive force at home. However, the quickest way to destroy the home advantage is trashing officials and visiting coaches and parents. Ask parents and fans to show sportsmanship in the stands as a positive reflection of the team and community.

A new idea that I have been exploring is using our covenant system and form parent covenants to promote maximum unity and cooperation for outstanding home court advantage.

Trash talking is just what it sounds like... TRASH!

Attitude of Positive Leadership

We cannot control every political circumstance, but we can control our response to it with Political Risk Management. Political Risk Management calls for a positive winning attitude. A winning attitude is golden. Attitude direction is a conscious decision drawn from our personal empowerment. Good and bad things can happen. When something happens unexpectedly, we can choose to remain positive, making the best of any situation. Some of our best lessons come from living through bad times and situations. Adversity builds character when allowed, but adversity always reveals true character without permission.

Leaders learn quickly to recover from wins or defeats and continue toward positive goals. Positive leaders are never afraid to fail and know when to ask for help. For them, winning is a result of cause-and-effect principles. They learn more so that they may give more to others.

I witnessed the pounding of a local baseball team on their home field. In the last inning, the home team needed six runs to win the game. No one in the stands had any faith that the team could come back. Many fans had already made their way into the parking lot. I stood next to the dugout and could hear the team captain talking. "We made them look good for most of the game! What do you say now? Lets play some baseball!" The calm, yet powerful conviction in that voice rocked me! Nothing, save a fire, could have made me miss the rest of this game. Each batter seemed to hold their bat like it was a part of their body, something missing earlier. Each young man that took a turn at the plate displayed body language that said winner! I witnessed one of the greatest comebacks in the school's history. The home team won a victory over the number one-rated team in their conference. The best talent lost that afternoon, but the best attitude won, although it came late. My favorite motto in sports is *never give up*!

Positive leaders working in political relationships learn to be secure with them, thus making it easier for leaders to discern, trust, and lead their teammates. With this trust, they can build positive relationships, including political relationships that maintain the discipline of the team. Teammates should associate good character, respect and responsibility as characteristics of winners.

Political Risk Management demands that positive leaders place the safety and welfare of team members above winning. Success is finding and creating the best environment for achieving the highest potential. The best leadership adapts to political relationship changes without fear. Leaders go the extra mile for their friends and all those for whom they are responsible.

Positive leaders are covenant makers and never covenant breakers. Talented people gravitate to positive leaders where they feel safe to participate and use their best skills. No one feels under-appreciated around the positive leader. The best leaders accept and understand the realities of the political nature of their position. Leaders know that relationships will have elements of the political and will act and plan accordingly.

Kobayashi Maru for Coaches

Definition: *The no-win scenario.*

The following are practice exercises.

P L A Y E R S	
	Head Coach Assistant Coach Star Player Parent of Player Team Captain

The Scenario: The state final's basketball game, half-hour before the introduction of the final teams, in a small locker room office, a heated meeting begins. The Team Captain has accused the Star Player of drinking alcohol last night in the hotel. The media has heavily-favored the team to win the championship because of their Star Player.

Pick a role and solve the problem.

P L A Y E R S	
	Volleyball Head Coach Athletic Director Parent One Parent Two

The Scenario: Parent One accuses the Volleyball Head Coach of favoritism toward Parent Two's daughter who is the girlfriend of the Athletic Director's son. The issue is playing time on the court. Parent One's daughter is the better player, but Parent Two's daughter is the Team Captain.

Pick a role and solve the problem.

P
L
A
Y
E
R
S

Head Coach
Assistant Coach
Star Player

The Scenario: The Head Coach has just announced that he is leaving at the end of the season and will recommend his replacement at the end of his last championship game. The Assistant Coach, who is the leading candidate, discovers that the Star Player's (quarterback) eligibility status is in error. The quarterback is really ineligible for this game and only he knows. What should be done?

Pick a role and solve the problem.

P
L
A
Y
E
R
S

Two Wrestling
    Team Captains
Varsity Club
    President
Wrestler
    (Defending
    State Champ)

The Scenario: Varsity Club President witnessed a rules violation of the Star Wrestler. He knows that the violation breaks the Varsity Club rules and they would remove the wrestler from the club and the wrestling team. The dilemma is that the Varsity Club President is the Wrestler's backup. Will he reveal what he knows to the other Team Captains or the coach?

Pick a role and solve the problem.

P
L
A
Y
E
R
S

Head Coach
First Assistant
    Coach
Second Assistant
    Coach)

The Scenario: It's the homecoming game and the Head Coach needs to win this game against their biggest rival and to win the conference to keep his job. Second Assistant Coach discovers three days before the game, that the Head Coach and First Assistant Coach have obtained the stolen game plan of the rival team. What should the Second Assistant Coach do?

Pick a role and solve the problem.

Chapter Seven

Applied Political Risk Management

Applied Political Risk Management is the process of managing active political situations. The absolute best way to stay out of terminal political situations is through preventive Political Risk Management; however, when pre-existing conditions and problems arise and we find ourselves inheriting someone else's trouble, then we need to carry out Applied Political Risk Management (APRM). APRM is a model for problem-solving pre-existing political problems.

Before going any further, I must make a few term distinctions. Receiving advice and receiving counsel are two very different processes worth noting.

- When we have empowered an advisor to give advice, he/she has taken the responsibility to discern and sort out our thoughts making decisions that we must live with or die. In effect, we have transferred personal empowerment to someone else. In ancient times, when the king took an advisor's advice, both risked much and if the advice were bad...death to the advisor. Avoid this situation as much as possible.

- In contrast, counseling offers several best alternatives with their related logical implications. The object of this method is to define the field of choices available. Leaving the specific choice up to us so we maintain our power of choice or personal empowerment (a much better choice most of the time).

- Sometimes, professional athletes fall victim to the financial advisor. Many a boxer had their fortunes squandered and mismanaged by a financial advisor. These victims paid a price by giving up their personal empowerment to someone else. Therefore, for whatever we seek advice, know that the risk can be serious. Most who seek the help of an advisor forget that advice given *does not have to be advice* taken.

When taking over a new position, inevitably pre-existing problems and potentially negative political situations soon appear to darken the day.

Political Management for Athletic Directors

The athletic director's job is usually rife with political fires and always short on timely information. Athletic directors are always last to know about their own political welfare, especially without Political Risk Management. One size does not fit all when it comes to political wisdom and political protection. As a consultant, I have encouraged athletic directors to use the following strategy-winners under various political circumstances.

Public Sports Counseling Panel—a group of people from the community meant to serve as an information panel for the athletic director (note: listening to advice is different from having to accept it).

The main purpose of the Public Sports Counseling Panel is to bring ideas and issues that concern the athletic program to the attention of the Athletic Director. This can be the best way to help athletic directors to learn directly the political balance and issues within the community. Getting to the real interest and concerns early is playing it smart. When forming such a panel, first specify clear guidelines. We must carefully plan guidelines as to specific empowerment of this Sports Counseling Panel as a group and as individuals. This group must understand plainly the scope, purpose, and length of a term. Athletic directors should regulate the appointment of such members. Stacking the panel with potential political fire starters and political critics makes for smart politics. This panel must not discuss sports policy and failure to make and enforce this absolute rule could make the athletic director the creator of his/her own Frankenstein monster. We know what happened to the doctor in the end! I do not recommend using the title *board* in describing the Sports Counseling Panel. Some over-involved individuals consumed with their own importance, fly like pigeons in the lofty clouds dropping a mess onto your beautiful, fresh program. Select the critics and those that profess to know the job better than the athletic director does for this panel, and a few connected people. If the athletic director is a good listener, this panel could be a gold mine for useful political information. Knowledge of the motives, perceptions and beliefs of power-group members are extremely valuable, but never for manipulation, only for effective communications. For the record, any form of manipulation is negative and will produce negative effects.

Sports Counseling Team — *the athletic director's personal and private sports counseling team.*

Not connected to any local power groups, this small experienced group of trusted and experienced friends can help us stay objective and help support us through tough times. Confiding important confidences to people with whom we have active political responsibilities is almost impossible. Good friends help us to stay honest with ourselves and are willing to tell us that we may be right or wrong. Friends can help lessen the stress of leadership. This team of friends can act as a group or be an individual according to need.

E-mail Access from the Public

Athletic directors must allow some near-instant responses to know the hot issues before they become rumor fodder and lethal political bullets. Remember that what we do not know politically can hurt and destroy us politically, making us somebody's liability. E-mail makes a paper record for further study and sometimes affords some legal protection. Angry fans or parents will have a quick way to vent without confronting us, thus avoiding some nasty compulsive violence. Over-involved parents left to fester their anger can generate a wave of negativity that can swell to tidal wave proportions in a matter of hours.

Coaches Covenant—*a verbal and written agreement to achieve specific goals while identifying responsibilities, commitment, and accountability through unity.*

Some risk-management experts have defined Coaches Covenants as a legal safety net. To know your coaches have a common commitment, unity, and accountability for responsibility is golden. Coaches will help police themselves when committed to a plan and purpose in which they feel real ownership. I have listed some best advantages of a Coaches Covenant:

a. Covenants can help the program avoid the worst negative baggage contamination from new or experienced coaches coming from other programs in worse shape than yours.

b. Covenants create a specific in-season job description that will help protect, both politically and legally, the coach, the athletic director, student athlete, and the program.

c. Covenants develop important unity and safety within the ranks of coaches for personal growth and professional development.

d. Non-teaching coaches and volunteer coaches will unite through the Coaches Covenant that links all other coaches together in the system. The continuity of philosophy, motive, and policy will bond all the coaches together into a real team. This also represents a blanket of political and legal protection for volunteer coaches and the entire athletic program.

e. Covenants provide a fair method of evaluating accountability and progress of your coaches and their teams.

More Political Management for the Athletic Director

Competent and loyal staff members are important. Let us start with the Athletic Secretary. Make peace with good secretaries, they

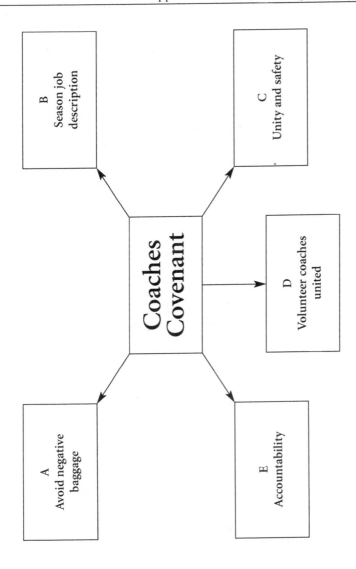

Figure 8

are the glue that daily holds the office together. Fight for better pay if necessary for them. Any good done to them will have positive returns to your program. Be careful selecting the person to occupy this vital position. Most institutions I have observed are very stingy when it comes to athletic secretary's numbers and pay. If we only have one, then shoot for the best.

Athletic directors must establish strong, positive communication with the maintenance supervisor and his/her crew. Show me a school with beautiful facilities and I will point out a good maintenance superintendent and crew. Giving public credit earned by maintenance is just and politically wise.

Alumni or booster clubs need the athletic director's special attention. Making friends with these groups can make any department look politically great. These groups can provide bodies at home sporting events and when the program needs it, voluntary help. Members of this group often lead important projects for the athletic department.

Teachers or instructors are an important power group that athletic directors often fail to take into proper account. This usually ends badly for the head coaches and student athletes. Academics rank number one in our learning institutions. Student athletes have a necessary connection to this power group. Make an enemy of teachers and student athletes will be the ones to suffer. The student athlete is a *shared* treasure that can become the system's most frequent victim in a power struggle between sports and academics. We should apply cautions when dealing with teachers because some are active opponents of athletics. National data shows that, overall, athletes are good students.

Having a good friend in the local paper's sports department can be a career saver, too. Learning individual likes and dislikes can make a difference in quality and quantity of issues that they report in the media. Truth and consistency are important traits when working with the media. A reputation of consistently holding the high ground of truth in a public conflict will serve the athletic director in gold. Most critics are reluctant to rip up a leader that habitually has the truth in his corner.

Political Management for Head Coaches

Many political management tools the athletic director uses are equally helpful to the head coach. Because parents are the number one antagonists of coaches, we should take some thought to look at issues relating to them. Parents need ownership in the program though sometimes they demand too much influence. Remember, when we see the word *influence*, it automatically becomes political.

The emotional influence of the parent on the student athlete can be problematic. Parents can tear at the athlete, pressuring the student between two authority figures—the coach and themselves. When the child is younger, the parent begins coaching their child from the stands. What can be more confusing than to try to listen to your coach over the heated cries of a domineering father or over-involved mother? Remember parents have a very strong emotional relationship that we should not underestimate. Parents represent the fieriest political catalysts. As a result, coaches have burned up like kindling wood under the heat.

Parent Responses. There are various methods to receiving opinions. The fastest, easiest, and most personal method is the most desirable as they serve hot issues and especially negative criticism more quickly and directly. Without quick-response capabilities, parents will call and rally other parents, creating a potential political crisis. By means of political pressure, angry parents represent the highest percentage of forced firing for athletic directors and head coaches. Championship coaches have found themselves fighting for their professional lives when opposed by a group of disenchanted parents. No one idea is right for every coach and community. Experiment and use the ones that work most consistently for your needs. One very successful high school football coach reviews his game film with the fathers of his athletes on a regular weekly schedule. Some use printed parental guidelines issued in the beginning of the season. Special parent meetings with the coach during the season have worked for some.

Team Covenants are oral and written agreements originally created by the athletes and coaches, establishing the goals, rules, responsibilities and penalties for all members. Well-written Team Covenants are the best protection and guides for handling potentially explosive, internal team issues like practice commitments and individual and team goals. Politically, good Team Covenants can be the best protection from political bullets shot by angry, overly-involved parents including disputes over playing time, which is probably at the top of the list for parent-coach confrontations.

Web Page Access can be very helpful in understanding the perception the community has about your team and program. The computer can help free the athletic director's secretary from fielding telephone questions that the athletic department can easily post to the web page, including important meetings or scheduled games or events, game results, fund raisers, etc.

Coaches Covenants are written agreements in which are listed the responsibilities, objectives, goals, and commitments level of coaches. Being part of a Coaches Covenant will link all your assistants and volunteer coaches into one unit. Accountability, safety, and unity are the target results. Sharing the top athletes in the school can go on smoothly from coach to coach. Coaches best benefit from the system's wealth of athletic talent and leadership through a covenant. By sharing, they all succeed without suspicion or mistrust in the coaching ranks. Politically safe environments produce the highest returns in coaching performance. Mentor programs for young coaches do not work where the unity of established coaches is failing. Everyone must actively be involved in the covenant system. Coaches, who do not like team commitment in their own house, cannot expect it from their student athletes.

Continuing Education demands that we stay current! Go to that conference that affects your sport. Ask your athletic director to subscribe to publications that influence your sport. Never rely on just our years of experience, the game is always changing and maybe we have not changed as swiftly. Do not fear innovation, big rewards come to the courageous Innovators. In high school sports, the Innovator has normally at least a full season's advantage over their opponents. Making major adjustments during a high school season is harder because of obvious time restrictions and varied levels of team talent. Therefore, a football coach with a successful major innovation in its offense and defense could run the table in the first season. Copycats seldom have the success of the original Innovator. Nevertheless, the Innovator will continue innovating, always staying ahead of other programs. Just when the opponent thinks they have a handle on last year's innovations, something new challenges them again. Be careful though, too much innovation could have a negative effect.

Lastly, make sure that the coaching job is really the right job. The talent and money might be right, but the politics could be quite deadly. Sometimes the coaching pool that one must work from is full of burned-out, tired rebels looking for a person to blame. The best coach in the world will say that they must have good help to succeed (see Chapter Five, *Selecting the Right Person for the Right Job*).

Political Survival in Conflict

Applied Political Risk Management should be used when political fires are directed at our position or us.

Case Study:

A small Midwest school district in the distant past had a great sports tradition. The district was now running their athletic programs with a series of part-time assistant principal/athletic directors. They had never hired a full-time athletic director. Twenty-five years after the winning tradition had died, especially football, they hired their first full-time professional athletic director to make positive changes.

During the years of mediocrity, the superintendent, and a few aggressive members of the school board, were directly influencing or controlling the daily operations of the athletic department, including the hiring and firing of head coaches, etc. In the past, the part-time athletic director had little support or empowerment in the job and that was the way some administrators wanted it. When they hired the full-time athletic director, he took over all daily duties as a regular part of his position.

When the position of head coach in football became vacant, the trouble started. The superintendent, the principal, and a school board member directly tried to install their own candidate in a secret deal. The athletic director declined to go along with this deception. He informed the administrators that the professional and right way to get a competent head coach was to create a fair method of choosing a candidate. Angered they agreed, but made the success or failure of the candidate as grounds for the athletic director's future employment/dismissal. Shortly after this incident, the superintendent told the athletic director not to attend certain administration and board meetings, a preface to dismissal.

In this situation, the misuse of empowerment, including gross conflict of interest, the "crapulization" of program needs, and narrow self-interest was poisoning the system. These preexisting problems proved too much for the athletic director.

> *We are responsible for what we say and what we do.*
> *We cannot change others.*
> *What we truly have ownership; we are responsible.*
> *What ever we have ownership over, we can improve or change.*

The following is a procedure to use to help resolve conflict in management by organizing our thinking.

Hint: *Write down the things understood about the problem.*

If we cannot write down the problem in a short paragraph, then we have not understood the problem. Gather more information and then start this process again. Writing down our thoughts will force us to organize our thinking and reveal the level of our understanding. The quality of the questions asked measure the real intelligence and understanding. Almost anybody can give an answer, even a fool, but few know how to ask good, answerable questions. Asking good questions requires knowledge. Often the reason that we repeatedly hammer our heads against the proverbial brick wall is because we failed to ask the right questions. Answers are often right in front of our face, but we are unable to see them because of the way we formed the question.

Case Study:

A friend of mine, a high school athletic director, called me in desperation, wanting to know what more he could do himself to save his job and win the support of the superintendent and the school board. Rumors that his job was in jeopardy had hit him hard. He had analyzed and scrutinized every possible thing about himself and could not find any obvious deficiencies. His last annual evaluation was good, meeting the goals set down by the principal and the superintendent. Finding no answers was driving him up the walls with sleepless nights. He lay in bed, staring at the ceiling wondering.

Listening very closely, to what he was saying, I told him that we could discover the truth. I did a little research and discovered what it was—the truth was that he was asking the wrong question. Therefore, no answer was possible to fit his question. Absolutely nothing was wrong with him! He was doing his duties to the letter as they had originally directed. Officially, the administration considered him a real asset and that is why they had originally hired him. However, the superintendent, and some board members, had not counted on the position of a full-time athletic director becoming such a visible and powerful political force. The athletic director's job was blocking the free wheeling-and-dealing in the athletic department by certain administrators and board members.

For years, some members of the administration and school board had used the head coaching positions as political levers for influence and favors. Hiring a full-time athletic director changed the dynamics. As a result, the athletic director's job had become a political liability to a powerful voting block on the school board. Now that he understood the nature of the political game, he could overcome the stress and internal pressure of not knowing. Eventually, the athletic director left his position for a new position that better suited his political skills and received better pay.

I will share some ideas with athletic directors and head coaches how to handle political conflict on the job.

Get Understanding. The order of this understanding is important. We must view any problem as a positive challenge and not as an overwhelming hurdle. This keeps the mind sharp and positive, sensitive to any subtle changes to important factors. Make sure that we understand and hold the high ground of truth in any conflict. Understand your own empowerment before dealing with others. Not understanding and using personal empowerment could create a no-win scenario leaving us feeling hopelessly trapped.

Another part of the problem with conflict is facing something new with almost no experience. Fear sets in! Fear can knot and cramp the mind, like a child's stomach packed full of green apples. The mind is a wondrous thing that we are now only beginning to suspect its potential. Understanding how we really work and what tools are ours to command is critical to our well being. Using the subconscious system can help in overcoming fears. Our subconscious mind cannot distinguish between what is real and what is not. The subconscious system literally believes whatever is presented strongly and repeatedly to it as a real event. Properly rehearsing problem-solving techniques as a mental exercise is the same as doing it for our subconscious system. Thinking positively will generate positive action. Our skill levels can increase dramatically when using this technique. We can prepare our thinking system to anticipate and act skillfully in a real crisis as if we had experience. This experience can displace many fears.

The Dynamics of Cause and Effect is one of the working principles that the subconscious mind uses to affect the relationship of belief translating to action. We think the first cause—what we think will affect what we say and do. Positive causes will generally yield positive effects. Negative causes will generally yield negative effects. Sometimes the seeker is asking the problem-solver for a temporary solution. The seeker may not really want to address the first cause, but is looking only for a remedy that deals with a specific effect.

Case Study:

> A principal and I were eating lunch when he leaned over the table and, with a very serious-sounding voice, asked me the question. How can we get more minority students to participate in our athletic department? Being familiar with this city, I had already understood some of its political and social dynamics. Still, I questioned him until I knew what he really wanted and would accept from me. I could have told him that the root solution involved wholesale changes in attitude away from general cultural bigotry in the community. However, what I told my friend is what he was prepared to receive. He really wanted to get more minorities on the football team this year, addressing only this specific part of the problem. He wanted the bandage, not the surgery.

The first cause meant extensive surgery, cutting things out and adding new positive thoughts and actions. In contrast, the principal only wanted a bandage approach to stop some bleeding. The burden for understanding these distinctions is on the problem-solver who is not always going to get clarity and honesty from those seeking solutions. Problem-solvers must question the seeker until they are sure what the real target is, the cause or the effect. Remember few know how to ask answerable questions, so the burden falls upon the problem-solver to make sure they can answer the form of the question given. It is also true that the principal did not have the Positional Empowerment to affect any changes to the root cause even if it were the target. However, some employers may want answers regardless of their ability to positionally act. Obtaining the knowledge of the state of the problem-seeker's empowerment may be important to the formation of the questions and answers.

Years ago, while teaching a bible study class, I asked the group "who is the opposite of God"? Almost everyone raised their hand and agreed it was Satan or the devil. When I explained about the principles of cause and effect to them, I knew they were beginning to understand when they all grew silent. One brave young man stood speaking for everyone: if God is the cause, then everything else is an effect. Therefore, God has no opposites, for everything else is part of creation.

The Search for
Truth in Conflict

In philosophical terms, a *straw man* is a weak or confusing argument used often to confuse the real issues. Conflicts become prolonged and nasty because somebody cannot understand the solvable issues. Sometimes somebody really does not want the issue resolved. Conflicts involve motives and levels of understanding. We must recognize and comprehend both the motives and levels of understanding truly to resolve a conflict. If power, control and influence are any part of the motive of any party or action, then the conflict is at least political in nature.

First stage: Search for the truth of the matter; discover the root problem. If we think we know the root or *first cause*, we should not tell anyone until we have obtained the necessary information in the second and third stages. People often have to be prepared to receive truth.

Second stage: Understand the personal empowerment, belief system, and perceptions of everyone directly involved (we may need our observations from working with our public panel or survey information to help determine this). Effective communications depends on second stage information.

Third stage: Based on their positional and legal empowerment, determine what the probable response of those involved in the conflict. I have an entire chapter dedicated to empowerment issues in this book. Good working relationships depend on this third stage.

Fourth stage: Define the root problem for all parties—this is critical. The object here is to formulate a properly answerable question, where we can produce facts and truths from the questions offered. Bring the group together to inform them that they require more information before arriving at a solution. Ask leading questions—this is where you ask the right questions, knowing what the answers will be ahead of time. Failure to act will cause a vacuum that someone negative will soon fill with political spins and harmful posturing. The leader to this point may not be viewed as a neutral party.

Do not offer the answers at this stage, but receive and encourage more questions. Your vulnerability will increase if you are bogged down in this stage. In a messy conflict, generously, but positively, using our empowerment will help us appear confident, avoiding appearing too defensive. Preparing everyone to receive the final solution is the object of this fourth stage.

The Fifth stage: Formally find an independent *outsider* to gather pertinent data for the stated problem if the conflict involves all or most of the power groups and trust is waning thin. Trust is essential in gathering and evaluating important information. We need not fear the outcome if we hold the high ground of truth. Chances are we already know the answers at this stage; it is getting them accepted that makes the challenge. Outside experts may be the saviors in nasty, complicated conflicts between power groups. When a qualified outsider says it, most often than not, everyone will accept it. All parties should receive the expert recommendations and evaluation results in written form. The biggest mistake people make, when using outside people to run a study, is that they keep the process and the results private. Believe me, the more public the information is the better for everyone involved.

All parties must agree upon a common philosophy that most of the power groups adopt for any meaningful resolution, or planned action, involving all parties for success. Make sure we have examined and dismissed all straw man arguments in considering the facts. The last act may be one of the most important. Create an obvious ceremony or event to declare closure of the conflict, jointly and openly, to avoid harmful political spinning later.

Case Study:

> The superintendent and the principal approved of the hiring of a new athletic director. Administrators made the decision to hire someone to manage the program. The two most popular sports in the program were football and men's basketball, competing somewhere in the middle of the pack in their conference standings.
>
> A few months later, three members of the school board and some influential parents began to criticize and demean

the effort of the athletic director. This was the opening gambit to go after the superintendent and athletic director. A very vocal group of fans thought that the teams were not playing to their expectations. Meanwhile, another parent group voiced their support of the new policy that all of the kids had to play in the games. The booster club also gave high marks for the athletic director's leadership in their program, where parental and public membership and participation was at an all-time high.

Die-hard sports fans, in the stands, began verbally protesting during the games. This group informed school board members and parents that they were not going to continue to support a program that did not seriously want to consistently win. Their view was that only the best athletes should play if they expected to win championships.

At the end of the school year, the principal informs the athletic director that they may not renew his contract. Three power groups loved him and four others wanted him gone. However, the athletic director faithfully and successfully fulfilled all the responsibilities in his job description. Fighting for his job, the athletic director was eventually fired and the conflict politically weakened the superintendent.

Tyrannical Leadership

Tyrannical leadership is very direct and very controlling. It is the most controversial style of leadership. Captain Ahab comes to mind when I think about this negative leadership style. The following is a little exercise to identify the traits of the tyrannical leadership style.

We may be using the Tyrannical Leadership *style when:*

- We feel we are the only one with worthy answers.
- We are quick to form opinions against people and their ideas before fairly analyzing and examining them. We are uncom-

fortable delegating real responsibility to others and letting go.We are unable to establish and maintain positive relationships with staff, players, parents, or other coaches.

- We must direct, set, and define the free time, including off-season vacations and holidays, of those under our responsibility.

- We are reluctant or unwilling to share athletes and their abilities or leadership with other coaches in the program.*Our winning is the highest priority.* We model our leadership style after other tyrannical-style leadership.We meant "do as I say and not as I do."We are uncomfortable around other talented members of our team.We have persisting feelings of suspicion and paranoia of everyone's motives.Are we defining disloyalty as anybody else's differentiating opinion?We answer challenges by quoting all our years of experience as a response.Hearing or reading any of this offends us.

Up Side and Down Side

Tyrannical-style leadership is slow to die out because of some meaningful short-range advantages to this style.

1. It can generate the fastest rate of change in a losing situation.

2. It can control people and circumstances around them more directly.

3. Things may run very efficiently for short periods.

4. It can generate good consistent win versus loss records.

5. There is strong opportunity for self-promotion.

Usually the conquest for total control leaves the children and the long-term health of the program at risk. The Negative Innovator type usually opts for this tyrannical style to carry out their objectives, though Manager and Pioneer types may use this tyrannical style as well.

Some attorneys are very watchful for potential tyrannical coaching violations concerning coaching and student athletes. Where sports participation is considered a privilege in public schools, it is also reasonable to deduce that coaching is also a privilege—a privilege with real responsibility. Almost every major athletic association has identified tyrannical coaching styles as undesirable.

Politically Troubled Programs

What are the warning signs that our program is heading into trouble? The first step in problem solving is to understand the problem. The second step is asking the proper questions. In the field, my associates and I identify troubled areas by calling them *red flags*. Listed are some red flags for athletic programs with coaching problems.

Red Flags

1. Covenant-breaking leaders, coaches or captains.
2. Leaders reverting to *tyrannical leadership* styles.
3. Habitual losing or failure.
4. Rampant feelings of under-appreciation by coaches and/or athletes.
5. Resentment against the success of other coaches.
6. All parties on the team or in the program no longer communicating.
7. Formations of cliques and rivalries.
8. Having problems improving the program and recruiting.
9. When winning or success takes priority over the safety and welfare of the athletes and/or coaches.

10. When coaches are habitually angry men and women.

11. When most athletes are habitually peaking before their senior year and digressing as seniors.

Breaking Bad Patterns

When a vacuum appears in positive leadership, usually negative influences will rush in to fill the void. Chronic negative situations often attract and feed negative-thinking people. Disunity within the program causes negative posturing, which splinters performances on all levels. What happens in the community—good or bad—affects the athletic department, because the kids and their parents are part of the community. Fair evaluations become impossible and negative speaking begins to dominate meetings and the media. Chronic failure will prevail where no trust and positive leadership dominate. Without good political relationships, widespread disunities exist.

The solution lies in the infusion of more positive leadership, by recruitment or by retraining leadership. Those elements infected by negative thinking will have to convert to becoming positive thinkers or forced to leave the team or program. Positive attitudes and relationships will attract and keep more positive thinking people in the program. Coaches or players, the dynamics are the same.

Programs with a recent history of prolonged bitter failures are susceptible to giving away mental confidence and positive direction. The coaches or captains may talk positively, but act negative, mirroring the rest of the team when the team needs role modeling in games and practices. Leaders may act subconsciously on negative thoughts in direct conflict with their public posturing.

Case Study:

I had a chance to observe individuals on a high school football team that had not won a single game in three years. One assistant coach asked me to come and observe their pre-practice the day before a game, in the locker room. The team was impressive with their over-the-top eagerness to *kick butts* (their term) and make an example out of the other team.

For one and a half quarters, they looked and played like state champions. In the second quarter, they were leading by ten points when one member of the team fumbled a punt and lost possession of the ball. The head coach and his assistants puffed up like volcanoes and erupted on the sidelines. The officials called time while the officials took some serious heat from the coaches arguing over the possession of the ball. I took my eyes off the coaches to look at the players on the field. The captains were yelling encouragement to the players on the field, thumping pads. When they saw their coaches raking the officials and heard the screaming of the crowd, they took up a belligerent posture. Finally, the game resumed. The next play, the entire defense made mistakes and the other team scored on a breakaway play.

The team went to the locker room at half time hanging their heads. Inside the locker room, much shouting and angry words were spoken against the officials by the coaches and the players. They left the locker room with the captains shouting. We can take these turkeys! When the game ended, the team had allowed five unanswered scores and lost the game. In the locker room, the coaches blamed the officials but mostly the team for not playing harder. In the parking lot, the players were blaming the officials.

On the bus home, and for years to come, some players would blame and doubt only themselves. Years later, these boys will seek counseling from someone like me. The coach had succeeded in making football the most important object in their lives on-season and off-season, for some kids four years. How equal is the effort to bring real healing-closure before the athlete moves on through graduation? Sports failures for many kids become hidden long-term, life-eating events relived repeatedly throughout their lives.

The solution lies in recognizing and replacing a negative idea with a positive one. Confidence and inspired performances are as contagious as negativity. Positive people empowered and inspired with positive ideas are proper counters to habitual losing mind-sets. If a proper positive attitude and a little innovation were all the team needed to begin winning again, they had already lost by default. Leaders must lead by positive example! We enhance others' chances for success when we are personally successful. Talking with the coaches, I realized that, in truth, the coaches did not really believe that they could be winners. They had prepared themselves and their athletes for defeat a week before the game. It was not a conscious act, but a belief working in their subconscious system. Not one coach had seen victory in their thoughts or imagination. They could not give their athletes what they did not have—a genuine winning attitude and the proper mental attitude to succeed. All of the confidence uttered by the coaches and the captains were only on the surface. When they had to start digging down for more confidence and performance during the game, it was not there.

Often, at the heart of *Troubled Teams* are faulty perceptions. Political relationships that are not based on truth can conjure up seemingly unsolvable barriers to success. In the last case study, I found some perceptions that had poisoned the potential of the team and program: "We are too small a school to compete with them!" "They have always been better!" "We will never have the talent to beat them."

The solution was to break through to the real issues, putting them out in the open. By way of questioning and comparing facts and truth, discover what is really true or false about these beliefs. Often getting past the denial of negative thinking and behavior can breathe new life into a team or program. One key is to encourage joint ownership. What we take into ownership, we can usually make positive changes. We may find political problems masked as something else.

Sometimes using wrong leadership types causes team problems. Sometimes schools tragically interchange the Manager with Pioneer-style leadership types, creating a world where administrators, coaches, and staff members are unable to work together. This management error can produce a work place filled with daily suspicions and misunderstandings.

Learning to be patient and remain positive will make the difference. Sometimes, the wrong leadership type is in the wrong position.

Employers must remove leaders unwilling to adapt to change. Parents of athletes, especially minors, should always stay informed about who is leading and what teaching their children are receiving. Failure to carry out effective closure for the athletes by coaches is very irresponsible. This is a particularly cruel failure for athletes coached by tyrannical coaches. Tyrannical-styled leaders win their share of games, but rarely match the negative cost with positive gains for the children.

Team Covenants

A Team covenant is a verbal and written agreement that defines the goals, objectives, responsibilities, accountability, commitment, and penalties of team members (see Figure 9).

Team Covenants are designed to:

1. Define and accept everyone's responsibilities.

2. Ensure accountability and a positive method to evaluate progress.

3. Build and maintain positive relationships and team unity.

4. Define and share positive, common goals and objectives for the season.

5. Define all relevant team rules and relevant penalties.

6. Help build up and maintain respect for teammates.

7. Teach positive values of team unity, leadership and trust.

8. Define helps and supports should coach or team desire additional outside aid.

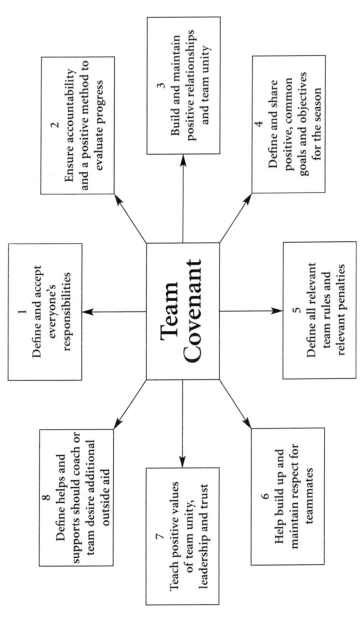

Team Covenant

1
Define and accept everyone's responsibilities

2
Ensure accountability and a positive method to evaluate progress

3
Build and maintain positive relationships and team unity

4
Define and share positive, common goals and objectives for the season

5
Define all relevant team rules and relevant penalties

6
Help build up and maintain respect for teammates

7
Teach positive values of team unity, leadership and trust

8
Define helps and supports should coach or team desire additional outside aid

Figure 9

Chapter Eight

Completing Risk Management

Defined: *Risk Management is the process of making and carrying out decisions that will minimize the adverse effects of accidental losses upon an organization*

[George L. Head, *Essentials of the Risk Management Process*].

Most universities, colleges and some school districts are familiar with Risk Management and, to these institutions, this could mean millions of dollars saved in lawsuits. From weight-room accidents to school bus incidents, Risk Management precautions saved money for these institutions. Stockholders have always understood the loss of resources as a political error. Now we consider the savings of resources as a political success. Risk Management failures are becoming political failures! Smart Political Risk Management helps prevent political failures by encouraging risk-management systems success. Remember that managing political matters on the job is an important part of management and leadership skills and duties.

The perception that an institution or organization cannot afford a Risk Management program centers around a belief that money, time, and other resources spent on Risk Management cannot be *politically* justified. Political justifications involve the motives and objectives of the institution's leadership. When most of the leadership is politically uninterested with Risk Management objectives, as high priority, Risk Management is not politically justified.

The willingness to accept the consequences of a no Risk Management program becomes a political decision based upon political motives with financial implications. To justify a Risk Management organizational plan requires a Political Risk Management approach to this *political problem*. The secret to Risk Management acceptance is its political acceptance. We should see Risk Management as a political element. Businesses and institutions have shelved and never acted on many innovations and smart ideas tendered by individuals. The way to achieve justification for any idea, smart or otherwise, is through political dynamics. Have you ever wondered why bad policies seem never to go away even when you know better ones exist? On the other hand, have you wondered why inferior products and ideas are selected over the superior? Whoever successfully manages the political dynamics, their views, inferior or superior, will be considered. Political ignorance can close the doors of opportunities to even the most brilliant thinkers and their ideas. Not the wisest nor the best ideas, products, or methods, but the better political manager wins in the political world.

We have already discussed how external, political events can have effects on finances. A change of national political priorities and philosophy can affect interest rates on loans; the availability of credit or the cost of doing business can change a company or an institution's business priorities. A business can go from maximizing profits to struggling to stay in business, and all from a combination of internal and external *political* decisions. Thus, the lack of a Risk Management program is a political failure waiting to happen.

Political Risk Management necessarily bond financial implications and political motives together. Political decisions already control making money, and spending money through an internal political system. The political prowess of a candidate for company president or CEO is a major trait which many corporations covet. Brilliant ideas and good intentions can be lost in the wake of bad political decisions and bad political leadership. A smart company wants a politically smart leader. One decade past, nobody talked about *political correctness*. Can we still afford to disdain office politics and political relationships?

This chapter is not an attempt to write the definitive study on Risk Management. Several very good books are on the market already: *Risk Management in Sports Issues and Strategies*, edited by Herb Appenzeller (1998); and *Essentials of the Risk Management*

Process by George L Head, Ph.D. and Stephen Horn II, CPCU. However, the one important idea missing in these books is the important implications of Political Risk Management to Risk Management.

Traditionally, we consider first the political implications of our ideas. Like it or not, we are all intimately involved in politics. *Power, influence and control* are directly part of our everyday world where we work or play. Schools like to plan programs and activities by first considering how the power groups will politically receive the program. If they are wise, Risk Management implications should be considered during this stage. We have observed that political relationships are necessary for the execution of certain functions, systems and even the activation of empowerment. Liability and loss imply responsibilities that, in turn, must suggest empowerment. We know the use of empowerment is always political. *The best use of Risk Management depends on its placement in the planning process.* The joining of Political Risk Management with Risk Management seems the most logical place to start in the program-planning process. Therefore, by linking Political Risk Management with Risk Management, this assures that we address both considerations at the very beginning of the process and not at the end of the process. End-solutions usually finish with unacceptable results and harsher penalties.

Political Risk Management and Risk Management

Policies—*definite courses of action using political rules that are sometimes legal. Good policymaking should contain Political Risk Management and Risk Management considerations during formation* (*see* **Figure 10**).

The typical planning scenario, for many companies or institutions, usually does not take into account existing conflicting policies, while placing the problem-solution model at the program or lower

Typical Planning Model

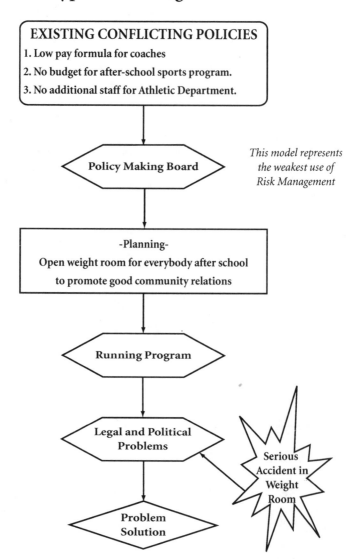

EXISTING CONFLICTING POLICIES
1. Low pay formula for coaches
2. No budget for after-school sports program.
3. No additional staff for Athletic Department.

Policy Making Board

This model represents the weakest use of Risk Management

-Planning-
Open weight room for everybody after school
to promote good community relations

Running Program

Legal and Political Problems

Serious Accident in Weight Room

Problem Solution

Figure 10

level instead of the beginning of planning. For maximum benefit, good planning must include all the best benefits of Political Risk Management and Risk Management in preventive problem solving before starting any activity or program.

When the Risk Management solution appears at the bottom of a flow chart for policy/program procedures, this can mean trouble because this represents the weakest use of Risk Management. Thus, risk-management solutions become more reactionary than preventive. Large legal settlements are typically reaching above six digits. This is a high price for simply poor planning procedures. Institutions cannot prevent all lawsuits, but Political Risk Management and Risk Management together may reduce how many and the severity of the penalty. First, good planning can prevent serious injury, major loss of all kinds of resources and provide the best safety possible. Second, sound Political Risk Management *must* include good Risk Management application in its most advantageous forms. I can think of no situation where this is not true. Prevention/planning management, using both ideas, makes the best sense.

Marrying the political motives with the Risk Management realities in the earliest planning stage will produce more realistic and balanced solutions (see **Figure 11**). Sometimes we have doomed the best-sounding activities and programs because political motives and Risk Management realities are not compatible enough. Better that these incompatibilities are discovered early and worked out before allocating and consuming valuable resources.

Look at it this way. Had the owner and captain of the Titanic applied Political Risk Management and Risk Management, both would have handled problems better. The dangers of sailing in the iceberg-filled waters would have been reduced. The possibilities of an accident would have generated more caution. This caution would have demanded the stocking of more boats and better training and preparations for the captain, crew, and passengers. Pure political motives powered the decision to speed recklessly through known iceberg-filled waters of the Atlantic that led to the disaster. The prestige of arriving early in port was the political motive. Poor placement of the Titanic's problem-solution produced deadly results—no one had seriously considered all the real possibilities.

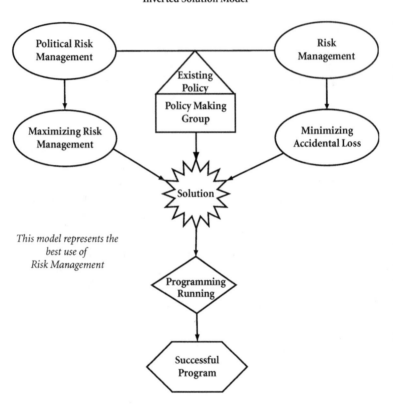

MARRIAGE OF POLITICAL

and

LEGAL RISK MANAGEMENT

Inverted Solution Model

Figure 11

Failure to join both the Risk Management and political motives in the building and operation of the ship led to one of history's worst disasters. Unfortunately, the builders did not design the ship to carry enough lifeboats for the number of passengers and the ship was overbooked. Later, after the sinking of the Titanic, authorities took some action, yet the costs for these late Risk Management considerations were unacceptably high in terms of human life and property.

> - All ships must have enough life jackets and boats.
> - They developed ways to track icebergs.
> - Better ship construction.
> - Mandatory disaster drills for the crew and passengers.

Question:

We may ask, while practicing Risk Management, will **we minimize adverse effects of accidental loss** on the political motives and financial objectives of the organization?

Question:

We may ask, while practicing Political Risk Management are we **maximizing** Risk Management to protect our political objectives and their financial implications acceptably.

Result:

The completion of both questions will produce clearer political and risk-managed paths to the most successful program or activity possible.

Political Risk Management does not limit possibilities, but manages the political and financial possibilities safely through Risk Management.

Let us not wait to act until disasters claim the health and resources of our organization damaging our political responsibilities. With the recent series of schoolyard shootings, can our institutions afford not to have Political Risk Management and Risk Management considerations? Through Political Risk Management and Risk Management, we can learn better to anticipate dangers and avoid costly waste. Maybe we will save our own lives and the lives of those we love.

Index